T0281826

ZANA FRAILLON

Zana Fraillon (she/her) was born in Naarm (Melbourne), but spent her early childhood in San Francisco. Her 2016 novel *The Bone Sparrow* won the ABIA Book of the Year for Older Children, the Readings Young Adult Book Prize and the Amnesty CILIP Honour. It was also shortlisted for the Prime Minister's Literary Awards, the Queensland Literary Awards, the Guardian Children's Fiction Prize, the Gold Inky and the CILIP Carnegie Medal.

Her book *The Lost Soul Atlas* (2020) won the 2020 Aurealis Award for Best Children's Fiction and was shortlisted for the 2021 Children's Book Council Award for Book of the Year: Older Readers.

Zana now lives in Naarm with her three children, husband and two dogs. Zana's passion for empowering young people to find their voice is a feature of both her books and her work with writers of all ages. When Zana isn't reading or writing, she likes to explore the museums and hidden passageways scattered across Naarm. They provide the same excitement as that moment before opening a new book – preparing to step into the unknown where a whole world of possibilities awaits.

S. SHAKTHIDHARAN

Shakthi is a western Sydney storyteller with Sri Lankan heritage and Tamil ancestry. He's a writer, director and producer of theatre and film, and composer of original music. His debut play *Counting and Cracking* (Belvoir and Co-Curious) received critical, commercial and community acclaim at the 2019 Sydney and Adelaide Festivals. The script won the Victorian Premier's Literature Prize and the NSW Premier's Nick Enright Prize for Playwriting; the production won seven Helpmann and three Sydney Theatre Awards.

Shakthi has in development a new commission with Sydney Festival; a number of plays with Belvoir; a feature film with Felix Media and two new TV projects. He's the Artistic Director of Kurinji and Lead Artistic Consultant at Co-Curious. Co-Curious is a sister company to CuriousWorks, where Shakthi was the Founder and Artistic Director from 2003–18. Shakthi was the Carriageworks inaugural Associate Artist and a recipient of both the Phillip Parson's and Kirk Robson Awards.

Zana Fraillon

THE BONE SPARROW

adapted for the stage by
S. Shakthidharan

NICK HERN BOOKS

London

www.nickhernbooks.co.uk

A Nick Hern Book

This adaptation of *The Bone Sparrow* first published in Great Britain as a paperback original in 2022 by Nick Hern Books Limited, The Glasshouse, 49a Goldhawk Road, London, in association with Pilot Theatre

The Bone Sparrow (play) copyright © 2022 S. Shakthidharan
The Bone Sparrow (book) copyright © 2016 Zana Fraillon
Introduction copyright © 2022 S. Shakthidharan
Educational Resources copyright © 2022 Pilot Theatre

Rohingya translations by Sirazul Islam and Mohammed Siddique
'Life is an Open Prison' and 'We are the People of Arakan' poems by Sirazul Islam
Bengali translation of 'Lor Chandrani' by Shamim Azad

Cover photo of Sirazul Islam by MSC1 Photography

Designed and typeset by Nick Hern Books, London
Printed in the UK by Mimeo Ltd, Huntingdon, Cambridgeshire PE29 6XX

A CIP catalogue record for this book is available from the British Library

ISBN 978 1 83904 081 8

Woodland
CARBON
www.woodlandcarbon.co.uk
NICK HERN BOOKS
Printed on Carbon Captured paper

Contents

Introduction
S. Shakthidharan

So often we are beaten down by the world. We reshape ourselves to fit into it. Subhi's story is different. In *The Bone Sparrow* this young boy discovers within himself a strength that will change the world around him. It is a classic coming-of-age story; and yet, so much more.

The Bone Sparrow is by turns a wondrous tale of epic, mythical adventure; a realistic appraisal of what it means to grow up without freedom; and a vision of renewed solidarity across our supposed divisions. These, to me, were the essential ingredients of Zana's wonderful novel.

The task of adapting it, then, was to present as boldly as possible these essential components whilst simultaneously assembling a grand theatricality around it all. This meant putting Subhi's diverse, complex relationships at the forefront of the narrative; and ensuring that Subhi's imaginary world and Jimmie's story within the story would reach the stage in a vivid and enchanting manner. But, most importantly, I wanted Subhi's story to be as specific and authentic as possible.

Pilot Theatre and I have worked closely with members of the Rohingya community to make this element of the work as essential as all the others. Their truths, hopes and desires, offered in a spirit of equal collaboration, were the bedrock I built everything else upon.

This adaptation of Zana Fraillon's *The Bone Sparrow* by
S. Shakthidharan was commissioned and first produced by Pilot
Theatre in a co-production with York Theatre Royal, Belgrade
Theatre Coventry, Derby Theatre and Mercury Theatre
Colchester, a consortium of theatres committed to producing
new and diverse work for younger audiences.

The Bone Sparrow is the third in a series of plays co-produced
by Pilot with these theatres, other productions being Malorie
Blackman's *Noughts + Crosses* adapted by Sabrina Mahfouz
and Alex Wheatle's *Crongton Knights* adapted by Emteaz
Hussain.

The Bone Sparrow was first performed at York Theatre Royal on 25 February 2022, before touring the UK. The cast was as follows (in alphabetical order):

QUEENIE/BOY ONE/ YOUNG ANKA	Siobhan Athwal
SUBHI	Yaamin Chowdhury
MAÁ/MIRKA/ZARA	Kiran L. Dadlani
ELI/HEAD BOY/SOLDIER	Elmi Rashid Elmi
DOCTOR/DUCK/DETAINEE/ BABY ANKA/ADULT ANKA	Jummy Faruq
BA/NASIR/HARVEY/OTO	Devesh Kishore
JIMMIE	Mary Roubos
BEAVER/SOLDIER	Mackenzie Scott

Director	Esther Richardson
Designer	Miriam Nabarro
Lighting Designer	Ben Cowens
Composition and Sound Design	Arun Ghosh
Video Designer and Illustrator	Daniel Denton
Illustrator	Maha Alomari
Puppetry Director	Alison Duddle
Staff Director	Júlia Levai
Assistant Director	Sirazul Islam
Movement Directors	Hannah Wintie-Hawkins and Drew Wintie-Hawkins
Fight Director	Kenan Ali
Dramaturgy	Oliver O'Shea
Voice Coach	Yvonne Morley
AV Programmer	Tim Kelly
Australian Accent Coach	Mary Howland
Rohingyan Accent Coach	Hetal Varia
Bangla Poem Consultant	Shamim Azad
Rohingya Consultants	Htike Htike and Mohammed Siddique
Production Manager (York)	Henry Thomas
Production Manager (tour)	Luke James

Company Stage Manager	Emily Walls
Company Stage Manager (*York*)	Anna Belderbos
Deputy Stage Manager	Denise Body
Assistant Stage Manager	Cat Simpson
Wardrobe Supervisor	Hazel Jupp
Deputy Wardrobe Supervisor	Janet Hull
Set Construction	Mercury Theatre Colchester
National Press and PR	Duncan Clarke PR

Special thanks to Ed Sunman, Gitika Buttoo, Cloud Islay Gallagher, Tiran Aakel, Komal Amin, Yousef Naseer, Manjeet Mann, Lucy Casson, Hirak Haldar, Regional Theatre Young Directors Scheme, Rosie Macpherson, SBC Theatre Company, Australian Theatre for Young People, and all the Pilot Theatre Young Associates.

For Pilot Theatre

Artistic Director	Esther Richardson
Executive Producer	Amanda J Smith
Company Administrator	Sarah Rorke
Marketing & Projects Producer	Lucy Hammond
Digital Officer	Sam Johnson
Finance Director	Helen Nakwhal
Creative Associate	Oliver O'Shea
Livestreaming Development Manager	Melanie Paris

pilot-theatre.com
@pilot_theatre

This text went to press before the end of rehearsals and so may differ slightly from the play as performed.

Characters

SUBHI (Subhan), *young male Rohingya, early teens*
QUEENY, *young female Rohingya, Subhi's older sister, late teens*
MAÁ, *older female Rohingya, Subhi's mother*
ELI (Elias), *young male person of colour, Subhi and Queeny's friend, late teens*
JIMMIE, *young female, early teens, Anglo-Celtic or European*
HARVEY, *older male person of colour or Indigenous Australian, guard*
BA, *older male person of colour, Subhi's father*
NASIR, *older male person of colour, Maá's friend*
BEAVER, *older male, any ethnicity, guard*
DUCK, *a puppet*

Other roles played by members of the ensemble:
DOCTOR
PETRA
HEAD BOY
ROUGH BOYS
ZARA
GUARDS
WORKERS
DETAINEES

Mirka, Anka, Oto and the soldiers are represented through a combination of masks and puppets, manoeuvred by members of the ensemble.

Setting

A detention centre in the remote Australian desert.

Note on the Text

A forward slash (/) indicates the point at which the next speaker interrupts.

Prologue

The dusty red earth of the Australian outback.

SUBHI *is drawing.*

He is drawing a story.

A bird appears – to his amazement. His ancestors come into being.

JIMMIE *enters, climbing down a tall ladder. The ancestors shift their focus to her.*

She holds a dusty box. She opens it. Inside is the Bone Sparrow necklace, which she puts on. There is also an old book – whose words she cannot decipher – and a paper boat.

As JIMMIE *plays with the paper boat the Night Sea appears and the boat starts to travel.* JIMMIE *disappears.*

There are people on the boat – people taking a long and dangerous journey. QUEENY *and* MAÁ *become the focus, clinging to each other.* MAÁ *is pregnant.*

This is SUBHI*'s story. The story he is drawing. The story he has heard many times before, of how they came to be here…*

Then MAÁ *screams and we shift to –*

ACT ONE

Scene One

MAÁ*'s tent.*

MAÁ. / Grrrrrrrrrrrr –

DOCTOR. Just breathe. Breathe...

> MAÁ *is giving birth. A* DOCTOR *assists her. She continues to growl and yell as the labour progresses; the* DOCTOR *continues to placate her – pointlessly.*

> BEAVER *stands guard.*

BEAVER (*into walkie-talkie*). It's happening now, mate. NAP-24. 24. You got that?

WALKIE-TALKIE (*muffled*). Copy. You said two hours –

BEAVER (*into walkie-talkie*). Yeah, it's earlier than we thought. Much earlier –

WALKIE-TALKIE. – the ambulance is at least thirty minutes / away –

QUEENY (*offstage, screaming*). LET ME IN!

BEAVER (*into walkie-talkie*). We'll have to do it here.

WALKIE-TALKIE. Copy. Report immediately afterwards.

BEAVER (*into walkie-talkie*). Copy.

DOCTOR. Okay – I can see the crown – / Push!

MAÁ. No! No!

DOCTOR. The baby wants to be in the world –

MAÁ. Not like this! / Not like this! No!

DOCTOR. / Push! Push!

QUEENY (*offstage, screaming*). LET ME IN!

MAÁ. He was supposed to be born free!

DOCTOR. / Push, goddammit –

> BA *enters, dressed in traditional Rohingya clothing. A figment of* MAÁ*'s imagination.*

BA (*Ruáingga*). Itare zito de maa. [Let him go, Maá.]

MAÁ. No!

BA (*Ruáingga*). Itare zito de. [Let him go.]

MAÁ. You aren't here yet. You don't get to choose.

> MAÁ *talks over* BA *as he recites his poem.*

BA. Life is an open prison
  We can see the sky and stars
  We can feel the breeze
  But we can never fly away
  The sky is the limit
  Yet we are the ground
  But I can still breathe the air of my motherland as it sweeps
    through the clouds
  One day we will grow wings and ride upon it.

MAÁ (*Ruáingga*). No matish! No matish! [Shut up. Shut up.] (*Starts pushing.*) Damn it. Damn it. Grrrrrrrrrrrrrrr –

> As BA *chants,* MAÁ, *still pissed off at BA, nevertheless begins to push.*

DOCTOR. Good. Good! That's it! / That's it!

QUEENY (*offstage, screaming*). LET ME IN FOR GOD'S SAKE!

> MAÁ *gives birth to a baby boy. The* DOCTOR *immediately takes the baby, examines it.*

DOCTOR. It's a boy –

MAÁ. / Give him to me!

DOCTOR (*to* GUARDS). All okay so far.

MAÁ. / (*shouting*). Give him to me!

QUEENY (*offstage, screaming*). LET ME IN!

BEAVER (*into walkie-talkie*). Boss. Boss?

WALKIE-TALKIE. Yes?

BEAVER (*into walkie-talkie*). He's arrived. So far so good.

WALKIE-TALKIE. Good. Ambulance should be there shortly.

    The DOCTOR *gives the baby to* MAÁ.

BEAVER (*into walkie-talkie*). Copy that. (*To the* DOCTOR.)
    We need to go and file the paperwork for DAR-1. I'm going
    to let the girl in now, yeah?

DOCTOR. Understood. Yes. Then I need to come back and do
    some more checks.

BEAVER. I just need your signature on a few things.

DOCTOR (*like he can't believe it*). DAR-1.

BEAVER. First baby born in the camp.

MAÁ (*holding her baby tight*). His. Name. Is. Subhan.

BEAVER. This way.

    As BEAVER *and the* DOCTOR *exit,* BA *exits also.* MAÁ
    watches him go.

    BEAVER *lets* QUEENY *in on the way out; she runs to her*
    mother.

QUEENY. Maá. Maá!

    They embrace.

MAÁ. *Futúni.* Meet your baby brother. Subhan.

    As QUEENY *takes baby Subhi and gives him a kiss, older*
    SUBHI *enters and watches them.*

QUEENY. Subhi. 'Our dawn'?

MAÁ (*nodding*). Our dawn – someday, Queeny. Someday.

Scene Two

The same tent, on the same red dirt. A sea-blue, traditional Rohingya fabric is draped at the front.

The dead of night. Everyone in the camp is asleep, except SUBHI, *who is drawing. He is now a young boy.* MAÁ *and* QUEENY*'s sweaty, prostrate bodies are beside him.*

SUBHI *draws the ocean. He draws feathers. The illustrations appears as hand-drawn animations, projected onto various parts of the set.*

A few feathers fall from the sky like rain. The sound of the ocean.

SUBHI. Sometimes, at night, the dirt outside turns into a beautiful ocean. The Night Sea. As red as the sun and as deep as the sky.

He looks at his MAÁ.

Maá says there are some people in this world who can see all the hidden bits and pieces of the universe blown in on the north wind and scattered about in the shadows.

He looks at his sister.

Queeny, she never tries to look in the shadows. She doesn't even squint. Maá sees, though. She can hear the ocean outside too.

He reaches back to MAÁ.

You hear it, Maá?

MAÁ *responds, talking in her sleep –*

MAÁ. Mhmmmmm…

As the feathers fall, the sound of a torrential downpour. There are whispers in the rain, whispers only SUBHI *can hear. He walks out of his tent, guided by them.*

Outside of the tent, rain falls onto him. His clothes are soaked.

SUBHI. Queeny says that when you swim deep down under the sea, you can watch all the fish and turtles and rays and sea flowers as bright as bright, and that you can lie on your back and let the sea carry you and you don't sink, not even a bit. The sea just lifts you up.

SUBHI *sees something on the ground. A seashell. He picks it up.*

BA *enters, his mouth moving. The whispers are his. They are in Ruáingga.* SUBHI *can't see him.*

BA (*whispering, Ruáingga*). Phunish, aar hota phunish. [Listen. Listen.]

SUBHI. Ba?

BA *slowly moves closer to* SUBHI.

I'm gonna see the sea. Feel it. Taste it. The real sea, someday. When me and Maá and Queeny are free. And on that day, Ba will be waiting there for us. On the shore. Won't you, Ba?

Scene Three

Lights change. There is no rain, no ocean, no feathers, no whispers, no BA. *It is daylight.*

ELI *enters. It's stinking hot – everyone's covered in sweat and their clothes stick to them.*

ELI. Subhi. Come on.

SUBHI. It's too hot to walk!

ELI. That is *exactly* when we should be doing our work. C'mon!

ELI *looks around carefully as he walks.* SUBHI *follows. They walk the fenced perimeter of the camp.*

There are fourteen pairs of real shoes in this whole entire camp, and close to nine hundred pairs of feet. If you want to keep those shoes of yours, you'd better start earning them.

SUBHI *looks down at his nice shoes, which are in contrast to his ragged, dusty clothes.*

SUBHI. And one day I won't have to stuff leaves and sticks and dirt in to make them fit –

ELI. That's right, bud. You're nineteen fence diamonds high now, right?

SUBHI. Twenty-one!

ELI. What?!

They high-five.

Growth spurt!

They walk.

SUBHI. Eli. Look what I found.

SUBHI *gives* ELI *the seashell.*

ELI. Another treasure?

SUBHI (*shy*). Yeah.

ELI. You still reckon this is your Ba. Leaving you gifts?

SUBHI. What else could it be?

ELI *puts the shell to his ear.*

What are you doing?

ELI *just listens.*

What do you hear, Eli?

ELI. The sea.

SUBHI. What?!

SUBHI *puts the shell to his ear. The sound of a faraway ocean. He listens, eyes wide.*

It *must* be from Ba!

ELI. Maybe, little guy. Maybe it is.

SUBHI. So that's what the real sea sounds like?

ELI. Yep.

SUBHI (*listening to the shell*). Wow.

ELI. My grandma used to tell me this story from a long, long way back. When the whole world was nothing but sea. This whale used to live in it. The biggest, hugest whale in that one big ocean. It was as old as the universe and as big as a country. Every night the whale would rise to the surface and sing a song to the moon. Her song pulled on the moon, and pulled and pulled, until the moon came close enough to whisper all its secrets.

SUBHI (*rapt*). What did the moon say?

ELI. That's for you to figure out, little man. When you listen to the shell.

SUBHI. Whoa.

They get to a particular spot.

ELI. Okay, bud. Work time.

SUBHI puts the shell away.

Remember. Never swap anywhere but here, yeah? Where the cameras can't see. If you can't do it here, just don't do it at all.

SUBHI nods, serious.

(*Gives* SUBHI *a package.*) For Nasir. Underwear. He says he can't patch up his holes any more. He's got a mozzie stick for ya. (*Another package.*) Petra. She wants to swap some washing powder for her toothpaste.

SUBHI. Got it, boss.

ELI. Don't call me that. We're partners. And…

He bends down. In this particular spot the bottom of the fence can be slightly pried apart and the earth dug up. With some subtle manoeuvring, ELI is able to put his hand under the fence, to the other side, and feel around in the ground. The sharp ends of the fence pierce his hand.

Ouch! (*Feeling around.*) Aha!

He stands back up, package in hand.

SUBHI. From our friends on the Outside?

ELI. You bet, bud. (*Gives* SUBHI *part of the package*.) Here.

SUBHI. Who for?

ELI. Pads for Maá and Queeny. When they have their women's time. Tell Queeny to distribute to the other women too, yeah?

SUBHI. Got it, partner.

ELI (*slips a package into his pocket*). And some toilet paper sheets for me.

> ELI *bends down and adjusts the bottom of the fence so it looks exactly like the rest of it.*

SUBHI. Why do we get more?

ELI. That's our tax for running this business in the first place. Understand?

> SUBHI *nods.*

Okay. Watch your back, little brother.

> ELI *exits.* SUBHI *waits a moment, then whistles.*

> *Another moment, then* NASIR *enters. He is an old man; a little bit mad. As they speak, they swap packages discreetly, without even acknowledging the action.*

NASIR. Subhi! Morning, son. Sure is hot hot hot hot?

SUBHI. On your way to breakfast, Nasir?

NASIR. Blergh! If you can call it that that that. Now when do I get one of those drawings?

SUBHI. When you finally tell me a story.

NASIR. A story a story a story story! Ah yes! But what story story to tell, Subhi? That is the question!

SUBHI. Any story!

NASIR. No! Never any story. Never any. It must be the right one. Do you understand? (*Exiting.*) Soon. Soon I will know, Subhi! What right story to tell tell!

SUBHI *watches* NASIR *leave with a grin. He doesn't see* BEAVER *enter.*

SUBHI *whistles again, and* PETRA *enters. She walks towards* SUBHI *with a grin, then freezes when she sees* BEAVER. PETRA *turns slowly, shaking her head, and exits another way.*

SUBHI *turns around, terrified.*

BEAVER. What are you doing here, DAR-1?

No response from SUBHI.

I asked you a question.

Still no response.

There's nothing here but fences and dirt.

SUBHI....I like fences and dirt.

BEAVER. Do you?

SUBHI....If I want to draw them well, I need to study them, you know.

SUBHI *walks away,* BEAVER *following.*

BEAVER....I don't usually come this way myself, except we got some important guests here today and they wanted to take a look around the grounds. Gotta check it all first myself, you know.

SUBHI. Guests? What guests?

BEAVER. What was that other detainee doing? Walking towards to you. / For what?

SUBHI (*closely examining a random bit of fence*). I – I can, I can draw you a fence, if you like –

BEAVER *pushes* SUBHI *to the ground, hard.* SUBHI *falls back with a shock.* BEAVER *stands over* SUBHI, *threatens to hit him.*

BEAVER. You're lucky we've got VIPs today, DAR-1. Very lucky.

BEAVER *searches through* SUBHI*'s pockets.*

And what do we have here?

He rips the packages from SUBHI*'s pockets and begins to tear them open.*

QUEENY *rushes in as* BEAVER *uncovers a mozzie stick and some washing powder.*

QUEENY (*to* SUBHI). Hey! I told you to go straight to the laundry! (*To* BEAVER.) He always comes out here to draw. I told him to go to the laundry to wash some of our –

BEAVER *is holding up the mozzie stick –*

You know how it is at the laundry. We get covered in bites just washing a pair of undies. Especially at this time of the month –

BEAVER *spits on the ground near* QUEENY*'s feet, and walks off.* QUEENY *rushes to her brother, picks him up from the ground, starts walking back to where* ELI *left* SUBHI.

(*Whispering.*) We saw him soon after Eli split from you. Sorry, brother. Beaver's not supposed to be in today. Got there just in time, hey?!

She acts like it's no big deal but we can see that QUEENY *is very relieved nothing worse happened.* SUBHI *gives her the package of pads.*

SUBHI. For you. And the other women.

QUEENY (*taking it*). Thanks, brother. (*Trying to distract him.*) Hey. I've got some good news for you.

SUBHI. What?

ELI *enters, and joins them walking through the camp, along the fence line. He immediately checks* SUBHI *for bruises, gives him a hug. He shares a look with* QUEENY *but they hide their worry from* SUBHI.

ELI. Sorry, bud. I didn't know. I would never have let you run if I'd –

SUBHI. It's fine.

ELI. No. It was my fault. I'm sorry. Okay?

SUBHI. Okay.

ELI (*checking the back of* SUBHI*'s head*). That bastard.

QUEENY. What?

ELI. He's got a little bruise there.

Now QUEENY*'s looking too.*

QUEENY. Bloody Beaver!

SUBHI. It's just a scratch. I'm fine. (*To* QUEENY.) What's the good news?

ELI. Yeah. You're a big brave guy, I know!

ELI *takes him in for another big-bro hug.*

Okay. This way, guys!

SUBHI. I don't feel like eating.

ELI. Subhi! Trust me. You'll want to see this.

SUBHI. What?

ELI. Just come on! You'll see.

They walk. SUBHI *shows* QUEENY *the shell.*

SUBHI. Look, Queeny.

QUEENY. What? It's a shell.

SUBHI. Listen.

She puts it to her ear.

That's the sound of the sea. The moon's secrets.

QUEENY. Pfft. That's just air swishing about.

SUBHI (*grabbing it back*). Give it back to me then.

QUEENY. Whatever, buttface.

They arrive at the mess. A table and set of chairs is assembled around them. SUBHI *sits at the table with* ELI *and* QUEENY.

BEAVER *enters, waiting, watchful.* QUEENY *and* ELI *give him dirties.* BEAVER *just laughs.*

A WORKER *puts up a sign for the meals that day. Breakfast is porridge, dinner is soup. But lunch is chicken and roasted vegetables and fruit salad for dessert.*

Subhi, look at lunch. Look!

SUBHI. Fruit! At lunchtime! Real fruit.

QUEENY. And real chicken.

ELI. And real vegetables.

QUEENY (*nudging* SUBHI). See? Good news.

SUBHI. But why?

ELI. Government people must be visiting.

QUEENY. Or the Human Rightsters. The food is always the tastiest when they come.

SUBHI. So that's why Beaver's on today –

QUEENY. Mmhm.

ELI. One day, when we're outta here, we'll eat like that every day, little bud.

SUBHI. Really?!

ELI. Even better than that! You know, there are places in the world that are so cold that you can't last an hour without freezing right up, and the only thing that can save you is hot chocolate so sweet and hot it burns your throat and thaws you out from the inside.

SUBHI. What's hot chocolate?

ELI. Sugar and chocolate and milk and more sugar all melted and / hot and –

SUBHI. No way!?

QUEENY *just shakes her head but* SUBHI *laps it up.*

ELI. One day, the two of us will be world-famous hot-chocolate chefs. I'll make it and you'll do amazing drawings in the milk.

SUBHI. You're crazy!

ELI. That's something people do!

SUBHI. Really?

ELI. Really. People will come from all over just to taste your
drawings.

They're laughing as a WORKER *comes over and serves
breakfast. It's slop. It's disgusting.*

SUBHI (*deflated*). Lunch feels so far away.

ELI. Just imagine it's hot chocolate, Subhi.

SUBHI. No thanks. I'll wait. (*Pushes the food aside.*) Queeny?
Tell me the donkey story?

QUEENY. Subhi –

SUBHI. Please! Just like Maá used to? Before she stopped…

QUEENY. Subhi.

SUBHI (*whispering*). We made a deal. I run the packages for
y'all, you tell me stories –

QUEENY. / Shut up!

ELI. Sssssh! For God's sake, tell him a story, Queeny.

QUEENY (*frustrated*). Once there was a donkey called Ansuro.
The end.

SUBHI. Queeny!

ELI. Yeah come on, Queeny! What kind of story is that?!

QUEENY. Argh!… In the village we grew up in –

SUBHI. Yay!

QUEENY. Shut up! In the village we grew up in – Me, Maá and
Ba –

SUBHI. When I was still / in Maá's belly –

QUEENY. When you were still in Maá's belly, yes. We had a
donkey. Called Ansuro.

SUBHI *begins to draw in his book.*

(*Grabbing his book*.) How many donkeys and stars do you have in there?

SUBHI (*grabbing it back*). There are other things too!

QUEENY. What, fences and dirt?

SUBHI. Just tell the story!

QUEENY. On special days, when we went swimming in the river –

SUBHI. Which was in the jungle, / at the edge of the village –

QUEENY. In the jungle at the edge of the village, yes. The donkey would follow us into the water. Donkeys don't usually like to swim. But this one did. So we called it (*Ruáingga*.) Ansuro. Swimmer.

SUBHI (*tasting the word*). Ansuro.

ELI. I've always liked this donkey.

QUEENY. We'd spend the whole day by (*Ruáingga*.) fossin haal, the north river. Baa would tell the worst dad jokes and we'd all groan but he'd swear he could hear you laughing from inside Maá's belly.

SUBHI. I'm sure I was!

QUEENY. And by the time we got back home it was dark, and the stars would be out. It was so hot we'd sit outside in our undies and on really special days like Eid, we'd do *qurbani*, and Maá and Baa would slaughter a cow. After the feast we'd lie down on the ground and look at the sky and wait for a shooting star. Ansuro would always bray when one appeared.

ELI. I don't believe that bit.

QUEENY. It's true, actually.

ELI (*tickling* SUBHI). Your Ba probably tickled the donkey's underside whenever a shooting star appeared.

QUEENY. Probably.

SUBHI (*laughing*). Did Ba do that kind of thing?

QUEENY (*suddenly sad*). Yeah. He did.

SUBHI. Silly Ba! What happened to Ansuro when we had to leave?

QUEENY. Subhi. You really think we had time to think about the donkey when the military came?

HARVEY (*entering*). Hose day today!

HARVEY *is struggling to carry a plastic pool in the shape of a giant clam shell.* BEAVER *watches him, laughing.*

BEAVER. You 'right there, Harvey?

HARVEY (*as he assembles the pool, ignoring* BEAVER). I've got a joke for you, kid. You ready?

SUBHI *nods.*

What do you get if you cross a chicken with a wolf?

SUBHI. What?

HARVEY. Just the wolf. The chicken didn't stand a chance.

SUBHI. That's not even funny –

HARVEY*'s laughing too loudly to hear* SUBHI. *He fills the pool with water.*

BEAVER. Wasting water there, mate.

HARVEY. It's forty-eight degrees. I'm gonna fill the damn thing to the top. Here.

HARVEY *passes water bottles to the kids and throws a plastic* DUCK *into the pool. The kids drain the bottles. He keeps filling up the pool.*

Drawing another story there, Subhi?

ELI. It's the donkey again.

SUBHI. Do you know how to say 'swim' in Ruáingga? Ansuro.

QUEENY. You're not even saying it right.

SUBHI. Yes I am!

HARVEY. It's okay, mate. You're our Aussie boy, don't forget that!

QUEENY (*snorts*). Aussie boy!

HARVEY. Nothing wrong with that!

ELI. You do sound more like Harvey than Queeny.

QUEENY. Even the way you walk is more like him than me.

SUBHI (*quietened*). Whatever. (*Keeps drawing.*)

    QUEENY *steps forward to the pool, picks up the toy* DUCK.

QUEENY. What's with the duck?

HARVEY. It's a pool. Every pool's gotta have a little duck in it.

QUEENY. This duck has a moustache. And a jacket. And a
    message under its wing – (*Looks.*)

SUBHI. What does it say?

QUEENY. To quack or not to quack.

HARVEY. It's a Shakespeare duck.

    QUEENY *stares at* HARVEY.

    He wrote plays – he's famous.

    QUEENY *throws the* DUCK *over her shoulder.* SUBHI
    picks it up. QUEENY *puts a toe into the water.*

QUEENY. It's too hot already. I don't know why you bother.
    With the pool – (*Looks at her brother.*) or with your
    drawings.

    She starts to exit, motioning to ELI.

    (*Exiting.*) Eli.

HARVEY (*sincere*). What's the problem, Queeny?

    QUEENY *ignores* HARVEY. ELI *begins to follow*
    QUEENY *out. As he goes past* HARVEY*:*

ELI (*motioning at* SUBHI). Check out the back of his head.

HARVEY. What?

ELI. Beaver. He threw him. Right onto the ground. Check it
    out.

SUBHI. I'm fine.

ELI. Who knows what he would have done or where he would have taken him if Queeny hadn't been watching out? But don't pretend like you care.

SUBHI. I'm fine!

ELI *joins up with* QUEENY *and they exit, throwing more dirties at* BEAVER, *which he laughs at.* HARVEY *watches them go, worried.*

HARVEY *looks at* BEAVER, *who shrugs. Then* BEAVER *gets a buzz on his walkie-talkie:*

WALKIE-TALKIE. Visitors are waiting for security clearance, do you read?

BEAVER (*into walkie-talkie, exiting*). Copy. On my way.

WALKIE-TALKIE. Copy.

BEAVER*'s gone.*

HARVEY (*to* SUBHI). You sure you're okay?

SUBHI. It's just a scratch.

HARVEY. Come here. Let me have a look.

SUBHI *groans but goes over to* HARVEY *and lets him check.*

Sorry, bud. I shoulda been keeping a better eye out.

SUBHI. It's fine really.

The pool is now full to the top and overflowing.

HARVEY. Ah! (*Turns off the hose.*) Here you go, mate. Your very own pool.

SUBHI (*looking at the sad pool*)....Thanks.

SUBHI *goes back to his drawing.*

HARVEY. Before you could even walk you were drawing shapes in the sand, you know.

SUBHI. Really? With what?

HARVEY. Really. With sticks. And rocks. You wouldn't believe how much paperwork I had to do to get you a bloody pencil. How much I still have to do.

SUBHI. Queeny says you never do anything like that for her.

HARVEY. Queeny wasn't born here.

SUBHI. ...Yeah.

HARVEY. ...Every one of your drawings is a story, Subhi. A kind of blanket to wrap yourself up in and keep you safe.

SUBHI. It's too hot for blankets.

HARVEY. A mosquito net, then.

SUBHI. They're just stupid scraps of paper, Harvey.

HARVEY. Yeah. But every little scrap joins up to every other little scrap. And one day everything will be covered in one gigantic mosquito net big enough to protect everyone.

SUBHI. A net full of every story there ever was?

HARVEY. And strong enough for every single person to hear.

SUBHI *smiles. Beat.*

SUBHI. Queeny doesn't get it. Everyone else in here has memories to hold on to. Everyone else has things to think on to stop them getting squashed down to nothing. But I don't have memories of anywhere else, and all these days just squish into the same. I need their stories. I need them to make my memories.

HARVEY *holds* SUBHI*'s shoulder.* BEAVER *enters, his walkie-talkie buzzing.*

BEAVER (*to* HARVEY). Oi. The lefties have finally decided to grace us with their presence. They're at the gate. C'mon.

HARVEY. Alright then. (*To* SUBHI.) See ya, bud.

HARVEY *and* BEAVER *exit.*

SUBHI (*watching them go*). Definitely the Human Rightsters.

DUCK. Definitely.

SUBHI, *now alone, looks at the* DUCK.

SUBHI....Hello?

DUCK. Well hello there.

SUBHI. What's a play, duck?

DUCK. It's not so different to your drawings.

SUBHI. Another kind of story?

DUCK. Mhm. Kid?

SUBHI. Yes?

DUCK. I don't like living in Harvey's garage so much. It's a bit same same, y'know? My suggestion is that I come and live with you instead.

SUBHI (*shrugging*). Okay, duck.

DUCK. Call me Bill.

The DUCK *snorts.*

SUBHI. Was that supposed to be funny?

DUCK. You don't get it. It's okay.

SUBHI *puts his drawings and seashell down and steps into the pool.*

The water's hot.

SUBHI. I don't care.

DUCK. Neither do I. But I'm made of plastic.

SUBHI *immerses himself in the water. The sound of the ocean, the rain and whispers return. A feather or two falls from the sky...*

Scene Four

Night. MAÁ's *tent. The women are inside, the men outside.*

The final moments of the evening call to prayer.

The prayer concludes. ELI *leaves;* NASIR *goes to leave –*

NASIR. Come come come. It is time time time.

SUBHI. Nasir? Nasir. What was that you were saying? Before? For Maá?

NASIR. Just an old poem poem poem –

SUBHI. Can we hear it?

MAÁ. It's time to go to bed, Subhi –

SUBHI. Please?! Nasir?

NASIR. I don't don't don't know it in English English –

SUBHI. Maá, do you know it?

MAÁ. Subhi –

SUBHI. Please! One story, Maá! To help us get to sleep.

MAÁ....Fine.

She wobbles her head at NASIR.

NASIR (*to* SUBHI). Okay. Until I figure out what story to give you, this will do. Hm?

SUBHI *nods, grinning.* NASIR *recites in Bangla and Ruáingga,* MAÁ *accompanying with her own version in English –*

boroshar ditio mashe

MAÁ. It rained for one month, then two

NASIR. anonde moyna hashe
        chole jolodhara ashepashe –

MAÁ. It would rain and rain and rain
        and Moyna felt happy –

NASIR. amje abeshe vore tar mon

MAÁ. Many moods flowed over her mind

NASIR. jol jhore vashe bishwo vubon

MAÁ. Like water flows over the earth

NASIR. chardik ondhokar rater rup dhore

MAÁ. It felt like it was only ever night, and

NASIR. nobo-bibahito jugol premkrira kore

MAÁ. The newlyweds were playing thrilling games of love –

SUBHI. / What?!

QUEENY. / Hahahahahahaha –

MAÁ (*laughing*). That's what the poem says!

SUBHI. Gross!

NASIR (*continuing*). puro ashman sobuj hoye jay

MAÁ. The sky? It is green.

NASIR. prantoro sobuje sobuje vore jay

MAÁ. The fields? They are green

NASIR. doshdish se roge rong bodlay

MAÁ. Green flows over the earth

NASIR. diner alo tatei purnota pay

MAÁ. Day comes and it is green too

NASIR. chole poromporay buddutrekha o megher khela

MAÁ. As lightning dances with the clouds

NASIR. premasokto buno-jugoler chole dehoros lila

MAÁ. Those lovers dance and make wonderful love

> SUBHI *makes a vomit noise, but he and* QUEENY *and all of them are laughing now* –

NASIR. raat – govir, ghono, o voyonkor raat ele

MAÁ. The night is fierce, endless and incredible

NASIR. tahatei kelikola o trogo cole – borne borne

MAÁ. The lovers and the colours flow over the earth

NASIR. sei pronoyer kale

MAÁ. And they all play

NASIR. vora borshar ditio mashe joltoronge

MAÁ. It rained for one month, then two

NASIR. susposhto veshe othe rritur agol sorbange

MAÁ. The seasons have shown themselves

NASIR. tora chara Hori, ki kore dei e vobonodi pari?

MAÁ. But where is Hori? Where is my beloved? How do I cross the river without my beloved?

The mood settles. They all thinking about BA. MAÁ *lies down in her bed.*

Come. Sleep.

SUBHI. He's coming, Maá. He's on his way. Ba. I can feel it.

Beat.

NASIR. You know, Subhi. That poem was was was written by your ancestors.

SUBHI. Really?

QUEENY. Duh.

SUBHI. Well no one tells me these things!

NASIR. Now I am telling you you.

SUBHI. If my ancestors wrote it, then how do you know it?

NASIR. The Rohingyans are more than refugees, son. They are poets and cooks and fighters and lovers and their stories are celebrated across the subcontinent and beyond. Everyone knows your people's poems. Your father is part of that that tradition.

SUBHI stares at NASIR *and* MAÁ *wide-eyed, taking it all in.* QUEENY *stands proud.*

Time to dream. Come come come.

NASIR *hugs the kids goodbye. He begins reciting the next verse of the poem and exits, dancing as he goes.*

MAÁ *closes her eyes.* QUEENY *lies down and does the same.* SUBHI *too, with the* DUCK *in his arms.*

They sleep, NASIR*'s dulcet voice still carried by the wind.*

But SUBHI *can't sleep.*

The sound of rain.

Feathers fall from the sky.

There are the faint whispers of BA *again.*

SUBHI *sits up. Looks at his sleeping family. Looks out at his Night Sea.*

SUBHI. Maá reckons that my Night Sea must pull everyone else's waking in on its currents and wash back deep sleep, nice and pure. Maá says it's because I listen to the earth. She says if everyone would listen to the stories deep down inside the earth, we would hear the whisperings of everything there is to hear, and if everyone did that, then just maybe we wouldn't all get stuck so much. Usually thinking on that helps me get to sleep, and then I don't know if the sea I'm hearing is the real Night Sea or just the one in my dreams.

But tonight, it's not working, Maá. Every time I close my eyes, I just see Beaver.

The DUCK *makes a noise.* SUBHI *takes it out –*

DUCK. I'm awake, you know.

SUBHI. You don't count. Your eyes can't actually shut.

DUCK. Rude.

SUBHI *shoves the* DUCK *back in his pocket. He crawls out of his bed and his tent, past the sleeping bodies of* MAÁ *and* QUEENY.

He walks around the camp, along the circumference of the fence, singing/reciting what he can remember of the poem. The DUCK *makes a noise again –*

SUBHI. Yes?

DUCK. Hello.

> SUBHI *shrugs his shoulders.*

> Knock knock!

SUBHI. Who's there?

DUCK. Queeny.

SUBHI. Queeny, / wh– ?

DUCK. Shut up, buttface!

SUBHI. Haha.

DUCK. Your turn!

SUBHI. Um – I don't…

> *…when suddenly he sees a girl,* JIMMIE.

> *She's at the spot. On the other side of the fence. Looking at it curiously.*

> SUBHI *looks at* JIMMIE. *She has a backpack on. She holds a big old book in the crook of one arm.*

> *She squats and pushes one hand deep into the dirt beneath her feet. She looks at* SUBHI *and smiles. She hocks up a huge bit of snot and spits in it. She tests something in the dirt again, then the fence. Then she stands.*

> *They stare at each other.*

JIMMIE. There's always a weak spot. Dad taught me. You just have to look.

SUBHI….Are you one of our Friends? From the Outside?

JIMMIE. What?

SUBHI….Nothing.

> *They stare at each other.*

JIMMIE. Do you lot have bikes in here?

SUBHI. What?

JIMMIE. Max, this guy at school, said he saw a container get delivered to the Centre, and inside it was full of brand-new bikes.

SUBHI. If that happened, they didn't give the bikes to us.

JIMMIE....Max is always making stuff up.

SUBHI. A bike wouldn't work in here anyway. Too many fences and tents in the way. And not even a single hill.

JIMMIE. Max reckons you get everything. Good clothes and thousands of toys and books and computers and teachers. Doctors who live right there in the Centre.

SUBHI....Oh.

JIMMIE (*looking up and around*). I wanted to come and check for myself. It didn't make sense. Why'd they put all these huge fences and barbed wire around it if it's so nice inside?

DUCK (*muffled*). She's a real talker huh?

SUBHI. We do have some computers. Queeny says they're pretty old. (*Gesturing behind him.*) They're on the other side of Hard Road. That's where all the hard buildings are, like the toilets and showers. But there are loads of people who are sick in here every day and no doctor comes to see them ever.

JIMMIE *nods*.

This is Family Compound. (*Gesturing.*) Across that fence is Alpha, which is where all the grown men without families live. Delta's for new arrivals. And Beta is...

JIMMIE. What?

SUBHI. Beta's where they take people the Jackets reckon are trouble.

JIMMIE. Trouble?

SUBHI. To others, or to themselves. They have extra fences and extra Jackets, and the Jackets have dogs.

JIMMIE. Mmm. I'm gonna tell Max that.

SUBHI....Okay.

JIMMIE. Is that your duck?

SUBHI *looks to the* DUCK.

DUCK. Where's this Night Sea? You keep promising me a sea. It's never been here. I need the water, you know –

SUBHI *shoves the* DUCK *in his pocket.*

(*Muffled.*) Oi!

SUBHI. He says you can call him Bill.

DUCK. No I didn't.

JIMMIE *gets it.*

JIMMIE. I have a pet rat.

SUBHI *grimaces.*

They're not dirty or anything. At least, Raticus isn't. He's lovely and smart.

Beat. SUBHI *doesn't know what to say next –*

Well, thanks um – What's your name?

SUBHI. Subhi.

JIMMIE. Thanks, Subhi. For the chat.

She spins and leaves, disappearing into the shadows –

SUBHI (*calling out*). Is that your book?

Pause.

Then JIMMIE *returns.*

JIMMIE. Course it is… Why. Can you read?

SUBHI *nods.*

Hm.

JIMMIE *opens the palimpsest slowly. She takes out a big black feather and twirls it around and around in her fingers. Somehow the moonlight reflects off it. Like it's magic.*

SUBHI *walks towards her slowly, wanting to touch her, to see if she's real.*

Bye, Subhi.

She spins again and disappears for good this time.

SUBHI *stares at the space where the girl was.*

He walks to the spot – and sits, alone.

DUCK. Glad she's gone.

SUBHI *puts his face down on the earth and closes his eyes.*

Subhi, gross! She spat there.

SUBHI *falls asleep, smiling.*

My eyes are closed now too, you know. Goodnight. Till it be tomorrow –

SUBHI. Ssssssssh.

The DUCK *sighs.*

Scene Five

Day.

HARVEY, ELI *and* QUEENY *assemble the mess hall around* SUBHI. ELI *lifts him into his chair; half his face is covered in dirt.* HARVEY *crouches down and looks at him.*

QUEENY. – he was just lying there, like his brain had melted –

The WORKER *serves miscellaneous porridge slop. On the board with meals listed is porridge for breakfast, soup for lunch and stew for dinner.*

Back to the usual then.

ELI. No one special here today.

HARVEY. What were you doing with your face in the ground, bud?

SUBHI. / Oh, um… I was…

QUEENY (*to* ELI). After breakfast, can we do our thing? That we said?

ELI (*nodding*). Of course. Everything's ready.

SUBHI (*to* HARVEY)....I was listening for stories from the earth.

QUEENY *and* ELI *snort. Even* SUBHI *laughs.*

Sounds stupid saying it out loud.

HARVEY *wipes the dirt from* SUBHI'*s face.*

HARVEY. It's not stupid at all, kid. Do you know that there are seven different types of dirt? You can tell a whole lot about a place by that dirt under your feet. All about people and animals and the / history of a place, just by—

BEAVER *enters, papers in his hands.*

BEAVER (*to* ELI). BER-18. Get up. (*To* HARVEY.) Think you're supposed to be watching this place, Harvey, not talking to kids about dirt.

HARVEY. I can do both.

BEAVER. BER-18. Get up. Now.

ELI *stands, slowly.*

SUBHI (*excited*). Eli! Eli!

ELI. Quiet, Subhi.

SUBHI. Eli! Maybe they're your papers. To be set free. Like when it happened to Amad, remember him? The Jackets came and his uncle was waiting at the gate and –

QUEENY. Subhi! Shut up!

But they're all excited – maybe this is ELI'*s time after all. To be set free.*

BEAVER. BER-18. Go pack your things. You're being moved to Alpha.

Shocked silence.

QUEENY. But that's for all the single men.

ELI. / But –

BEAVER. And don't ask me / any questions –

ELI. Why?

BEAVER. You're too old to be in Family. Move it, boy.

ELI *doesn't move.*

BER-18. *Move it.*

ELI. I'm still a good few years off going to Alpha, and you know it.

BEAVER *caresses* ELI*'s cheek with the papers.*

BEAVER. That's not what your paper says. Paper says you're nineteen. You were meant to move last week. And writing doesn't lie.

QUEENY *and* ELI *share a look. A big smile spreads across* BEAVER*'s face. He's got them trapped.*

QUEENY. Writing does lie. It lies all the time.

QUEENY *steps in between* BEAVER *and* ELI.

SUBHI. Queeny –

QUEENY (*to* BEAVER). You know what happens to the boys when they're put in with all the men, living together like that, without their families, without being able to work or learn or / do anything –

BEAVER. Shut up. BER-18. Now.

BEAVER*'s hand rests on the wand on his belt.* SUBHI *looks like he's about to cry.*

ELI (*to* SUBHI). Don't worry, buddy. Everything's going to be alright.

SUBHI. Eli?

ELI. Yeah?

SUBHI. Here. I think that's why Ba gave me this. To pass it on to you.

SUBHI *gives* ELI *the seashell.* ELI *smiles.*

ELI. Thanks, bud. Hey. We can still talk at the fence, okay?

SUBHI *nods*.

(*To* BEAVER.) It'll be nice to be in another part of the camp. Meet more of the people here. Maybe I'll learn a new trick or two from those men, hey, Beaver?

BEAVER....Move, BER-18.

ELI *blows* BEAVER *a kiss. He moves past* BEAVER, *walking defiantly, strongly.*

BEAVER. You've got five minutes to get your crap together. There better not be any trouble.

ELI (*as he exits*). Yes, sir!

BEAVER (*to* SUBHI). DAR-1. Tell your sister to stop pretending that she's more important than she really is.

BEAVER *exits*.

QUEENY. Thanks for nothing, Harvey.

HARVEY. Queeny –

QUEENY. Get out. Please. I wanna talk to my brother.

HARVEY. Queeny –

QUEENY. I said please.

HARVEY. I'm stationed here, Queeny. I can't go anywhere, you know that.

QUEENY. Fine.

She grabs SUBHI *and exits*.

(*Ruáingga*.) Aiyó. [Come on.]

HARVEY. Queeny!

She starts walking. SUBHI *follows*.

QUEENY. Beaver is such an ass.

SUBHI. Will Eli be okay?

QUEENY. I don't know, Subhi.

SUBHI. Queeny!

QUEENY. What? That's the truth! I don't know, okay?

They walk along the fence.

SUBHI. Queeny?

QUEENY. What?!

SUBHI. Why does Beaver hate us?

QUEENY. Some people are just mean.

SUBHI. That's it? That's why?

QUEENY. Kind of.

SUBHI. What do you mean?

QUEENY....You don't want to know.

SUBHI. Yes I do.

QUEENY. You can't handle it.

SUBHI. Yes I can!

QUEENY. Promise you won't be scared?

SUBHI. I'm twenty-one diamond fences high now!

QUEENY (*looking hard at her brother*). You know what? It's about time you learnt some of this stuff.

SUBHI. I'm ready.

QUEENY....So we're in the mess hall. Harvey is guarding us. And Nasir falls over. Real big clunk and chairs crashing and all – like he had a heart attack / or was choking or something –

SUBHI. Oh no! Nasir!

QUEENY. – Harvey went to help. Beaver was coming past and heard all the yells and screams, so he went to help as well. 'Cept when Harvey got closer to Nasir, this other fella –

SUBHI. Who?

QUEENY. You don't know him, Subhi –

SUBHI. But what was his –

QUEENY. He's gone now Subhi, okay?!

SUBHI....sorry.

QUEENY. – From nowhere this guy just got up and started running at Harvey with this hammer he'd been hiding. He was swinging that hammer *everywhere*. Beaver got in between him and Harvey. And hammer guy just... just laid into Beaver. Bashed him all over the head. Almost killed him, until Harvey managed to get the guy under control.

SUBHI. Whoa.

QUEENY. And that's why Harvey won't say a bad word about Beaver now. Spineless bastard.

SUBHI. Hey!

QUEENY. It's true, Subhi. Sorry.

SUBHI. So... Beaver saved Harvey's life?

QUEENY. I don't know. Maybe. All I know is, Beaver never trusted a single one of us after that.

They arrive at the spot.

SUBHI. Oh no, not here –

QUEENY. Yes, here.

SUBHI. But Eli –

QUEENY. We have to do it without Eli now, don't we?

SUBHI. What about / Beaver?

QUEENY. Shut up. Just wait here for a bit. I'll be back. I'll distract Beaver with some other stupid thing. Should be fun.

She goes to exit –

SUBHI. Where's the package?

QUEENY. What?

SUBHI. It's an exchange. I need to give a package to take one –

QUEENY. No. This one's different. It's from the Outside.

SUBHI. Like the books?

QUEENY (*in a hurry*). Yeah. Like the books.

SUBHI. Then why does it need to be a package?

QUEENY. Stop asking questions!

SUBHI. But Eli says we always –

QUEENY. SHUT UP. I'm the boss now, do you understand? And you do what I say.

SUBHI. Partners.

QUEENY. What?

SUBHI. We're supposed to be partners.

QUEENY. Subhi. Just do this last package, okay? And then I'll leave you and your stupid buttface duck alone for keeps. Understood?

She goes.

DUCK. I don't know why she had to mention me –

SUBHI. Shhhh.

SUBHI *waits for a bit. Nothing, He whistles. Nothing. He's about to go when he hears* PETRA *entering. She's as nervous as hell. She takes out a small package and gives it to* SUBHI. SUBHI *feels it to guess what it is. It's definitely not a book.*

PETRA. Tell your sister I'm not helping any more. This is it, okay?

SUBHI....Okay.

She exits in a rush. SUBHI *watches her go, then turns and goes back to his tent, nervous as all hell.*

QUEENY *is waiting at the tent.*

QUEENY. Why'd you take so long?!

She rips the packet out of SUBHI*'s pockets and runs off urgently.*

MAÁ *watches* QUEENY *run off.*

MAÁ. What's up her bum?

SUBHI....I'm not sure.

> SUBHI *sits down next to* MAÁ – *who is folding clothes –
> and helps her.*

> Maá...? Maá, Eli reckons everything is going to be alright
> but I have this feeling it isn't.

MAÁ....Elias is a smart boy. He'll be alright, Subhan.

> *Suddenly, a sparrow flies into their tent.* MAÁ *watches it
> closely.*

SUBHI. Whoa.

> *The sparrow looks at* SUBHI. *It looks at* MAÁ. *In the
> distance, the sound of the Night Sea rises and falls. A feather
> falls from the sky.*

> *Then the sparrow flies off again.*

> Wow. Wait till I tell Queeny! You know Harvey says that
> sparrows aren't from Australia, they were brought over here
> by people from England –

> MAÁ *is still looking the way the sparrow went, a frown on
> her face.*

> Maá?

MAÁ. For some, a sparrow in the house is a sign of death.

SUBHI (*frightened*). What?!

MAÁ (*embracing her son*). Hey. Hey! Death isn't always bad,
Subhi. Sometimes it is. Sometimes it's an end. But other
times... Death is a beginning. The beginning of something
new.

> SUBHI *takes it in. They continue folding clothes.*

SUBHI. Last night I met a girl from the Outside. And now I
think I dreamt her. It doesn't make any sense that a girl from
Outside would come here in the middle of the night...
Remember the other day when I dreamt I had already lined
up for my shower and when I woke I realised I had to wait in

line all over again? Maybe this is like that... Or maybe Ba
sent the girl. Whoa. Do you think that could be it?

No response; MAÁ *is staring at him.*

Maá?

MAÁ. I've got an idea.

SUBHI. What.

MAÁ. Why don't you see if she's there again tonight.

SUBHI....Okay.

They fold more clothes.

BA *appears onstage and begins to sing one of his poems in
Ruáingga. As* BA *sings, music plays and time stretches...
others from the camp join in.*

BA *(Ruáingga).* Añára óilam Arakanór manúic [We are the
    people of arakan]
    Añára dahàyum Araknor cúna sañdi [We will show the gold
    and silver of arakan]
    Arakanór ti duré óile yó, no búlium tuáñra [Even if I am
    away from Arakan, I will not forget you]

The rest of the company one by one join and sing with BA.

ALL. Ekdin añi górat aichum [One day we will come home]
    Ar rosúlór óu torikat uttum [And follow the teachings of the
    prophet]
    Zogot báci ré diuoum añara elóm ar ador [We will show the
    people our knowledge and love]

Overlapping with BA:

– SUBHI *picks up his pencil and papers and draws. A
ghostlike image of* JIMMIE *slowly comes together in the
animations.*

– *Upstage,* NASIR *dances and sings with* BA.

– *Downstage,* GUARDS *patrol past the tent.*

– QUEENY *sneaks in without speaking to anyone and goes
straight to bed.*

– *The sound of rain grows.*

– *Feathers fall from the sky.*

– MAÁ *falls asleep folding clothes.*

– *Day becomes night.*

The GUARDS *are no longer patrolling.*

The Night Sea is wild.

SUBHI *stands.*

DUCK. Do you really think it's wise to –

SUBHI. I could always leave you here.

DUCK….Fine.

    SUBHI *exits with the* DUCK.

    And he walks…

Scene Six

And he walks.

The moon is low tonight.

He arrives at the spot.

JIMMIE *is there. She has that feather again. She's twirling it, waiting.*

JIMMIE. About time.

    She stares at SUBHI, *sizing him up.* SUBHI *stares back.*

SUBHI. Are you real?

JIMMIE….If I wasn't, would I tell you?

    SUBHI *turns to the* DUCK –

DUCK. Don't look at me!

    Then looks back to JIMMIE.

SUBHI....Hm.

JIMMIE. How long have you been in here for?

SUBHI. Forever.

JIMMIE. What?

SUBHI. I'm one of the Limbo Kids.

> JIMMIE *doesn't understand.*

> I was born here. But they haven't decided yet where I'm going.

JIMMIE....What about your family?

SUBHI. I've got a sister, Queeny, but she's pretty rubbish mostly. And my Maá. She tells me stories of the sea. And my dad is on his way, but not here yet.

JIMMIE. Where is he?

SUBHI. I'm not sure, exactly. He was in prison, in Burma –

JIMMIE. Oh! What did he do?

SUBHI. Maá says it's because he's a poet. A Rohingyan poet.

JIMMIE....I see.

SUBHI. But he figured out how to escape, and he's on his way here now, coming to us over the seas. Maá promises. One day, we'll all be together.

> JIMMIE *nods.*

> And Eli is my best friend and just as good as a brother. Better than Queeny.

JIMMIE. How come you can read?

SUBHI. Eli and Queeny taught me. How to read and write and do maths. I've read everything there is to read in here. Magazines from before I was born. The folder with emergency numbers and names and instructions. And there's these religious people from the Outside who give us things like books and Harvey gives me every single kids' one that comes in.

JIMMIE. Harvey?

SUBHI. He's one of the Jackets.

> JIMMIE *nods again and stares at* SUBHI, *twirling the feather.*

JIMMIE. My mum's dead. She got this fever one time and something in her brain just popped, that's how the doctors said. And that was it. She was just dead, sitting right there on the bathroom floor.

SUBHI. Oh. (*Doesn't know what to say.*)

JIMMIE. I'm Jimmie by the way.

> *She puts her hand up against the fence.* SUBHI *slowly walks up to her and puts his hand against hers.*
>
> *They stand like that, close but divided.*

SUBHI....You smell real.

> JIMMIE *brings her hand down, pulls out a torch and turns it on.*

Turn it off! Turn it off!

JIMMIE (*turning it off*). Settle down.

SUBHI. Are you crazy?! Someone'll see!

JIMMIE. Well, where can we go then?

SUBHI. Go?

JIMMIE (*gesturing at the book*). To read my mum's stories. You said you could read.

> SUBHI *stares at* JIMMIE. *God, he wants to know what is in that book.*

SUBHI. Okay. But I hold the torch.

JIMMIE. Deal.

> JIMMIE *bends down and digs away at the earth. So does* SUBHI, *excited.*

DUCK (*as the kids dig*). Are you sure this is sensible? This doesn't seem very sensible. It's only a book of stories. I can tell you a story when you're nice and safe and tucked up in bed. Listen, here we go. *Spotlight! Two households, most alike in duck-nity, in fair Verona where we –*

SUBHI *shoves the* DUCK *deeper into his pocket.*

JIMMIE. After Mum's funeral Dad made us pack up all of Mum's stuff and put it high up in the attic. Her clothes, her pictures, her jewellery, everything. Dad thought that would help, not seeing anything of hers, but it didn't really. Anyway. That was when I found this. In one of Mum's boxes.

She takes a long look at the book and then carefully passes it under the fence to SUBHI. *The torch follows.*

They sit down in the dirt, either side of the fence. SUBHI *stares at the book with reverence.* JIMMIE *touches something hanging around her neck.*

This was Mum's too.

SUBHI *holds up her torch, covering most of the lamp with his hands, and turning it on. He shines it on her necklace. It is the Bone Sparrow from the Prologue. A shadowy image of it appears on the projections.*

DUCK (*scared*). Um... Subhi? Shall we get out of here?

JIMMIE. It's a sparrow carved from bone. Mum gave it to me just before she died.

Wind rushes through the camp. The red earth is unsettled. The animations appear again – and show feathers converging onto the bird. Its wings spread out and fly high on the wind.

SUBHI *drops the torch.*

DUCK. Eek!

JIMMIE *laughs.*

JIMMIE. It's not that bad. Although I guess her eye is kind of creepy.

SUBHI *picks up the torch and looks again.*

Mum said it gives us luck and protection. She said all the souls of everyone in our family, all our stories and everything, rub right into that bone and it keeps us together. But then Mum went and died, so...

SUBHI. So why do you wear it?

JIMMIE. I guess, just in case, maybe? Maybe if Mum wasn't wearing it, she would have died even sooner. Maybe it's a different kind of luck. I don't know, do I?

SUBHI *nods, then reaches out to touch the old book – it is a kind of palimpsest. He feels the front cover.* JIMMIE *watches him.*

SUBHI. Jimmie?

JIMMIE. Yeah?

SUBHI. Why can't you read?

JIMMIE. I'm dyslexic.

SUBHI. Dis-what?

JIMMIE. Dyslexic. I can do pretty much all the other stuff at school. But reading... when I see a letter on a page, it just looks like a picture to me. I can't figure out what sound it's supposed to make. And when I hear the sounds – I know what the sound is, I mean I could speak it to you, but I can't connect it to one of those pictures. I just can't.

SUBHI. Oh. Sorry.

JIMMIE. My dad is dyslexic. He can't read either. He's good at stuff with his hands, like fences and gardens and fixing all the stuff that keeps falling apart in our house. But not reading. The doctor back in the city used to say I got it from Dad. If I ever have kids, they might have it too.

SUBHI. Can you learn? Eventually I mean? Even if the learning is really slow?

JIMMIE. You can. With some people. But it was my mum that used to teach me.

SUBHI. What about school?

JIMMIE. This place is a million miles from anywhere, Subhi. School can barely get a normal teacher, let alone someone for a person like me.

SUBHI. Why don't you move? You can go anywhere you want, can't you?

JIMMIE. ...I don't want to move.

SUBHI. Oh. Why?

JIMMIE. Coz Mum used to love this place.

Beat.

Dad wishes we would move, though. This place is great for living near heaps of bush and sand and animals and stuff, but not so good for things like work and school and shopping. The only place Dad can get a job is as a security guard in the town. He works nights and we really only see each other on the weekends.

SUBHI. I wish I only saw Queeny on the weekend.

JIMMIE. But... if we leave this place. I feel like we're leaving Mum, y'know? Forever.

SUBHI *nods.* JIMMIE *reaches out to the book.*

This is all I have left of her. And I think... I think the stories are what matters, right? If I can't read them, I just have to figure out another way to receive them.

SUBHI. Sounds pretty smart to me.

JIMMIE. Good.

JIMMIE *closes her eyes.*

Go on then.

SUBHI *opens the book. He feels the first page with his fingers. He looks at* JIMMIE, *waiting, eyes closed.*

Then he reads.

SUBHI. This is a tale from long, long ago. Anka was found in a well.

JIMMIE. Anka was my great-great-great-grandmother.

SUBHI. She was left in a well. Who would do that?

JIMMIE. Beats me. Hurry up, will you? Stories don't work if you stop all the time. I thought you knew about reading!

SUBHI. Anka was found in a well.

A puppeteer enters with baby Anka as SUBHI *draws a well around them.*

No one knew who had left her there. But there she was. Halfway down an old well, on the outskirts of their village. Dirt sticking to her hair and skin.

A baby's cry.

Oto enters – a young boy – playing a game on his own.

It was young Oto who found her. He always played near there. He knew that no one else would hear the baby's cry.

Oto climbs into the well.

And so, he climbed – deep down into the dark… and rescued the child.

Oto climbs back out of the well, clutching baby Anka.

As he held the baby tightly, an undeniable surge of love filled his chest.

But what was he to do with her?

Wise old Mirka would know.

Mirka enters – old but sprightly. She wears the Bone Sparrow necklace. Oto goes to her, and gives her the baby.

Mirka could see that the child was blind. But she knew that Anka was destined to see more than most. She was already clinging to the Bone Sparrow around Mirka's neck, drawing in its luck and protection.

Oto circles Mirka and the baby, playing peekaboo. Anka can't see him, but she can hear him and giggles in response. Oto repeats the game, Anka's giggles growing louder each time.

Oto soon became Anka's favourite playmate. He vowed he would cherish and protect the girl no matter what she faced.

And sure enough – as the children grew, so did their love for each other.

– and then they are gone. SUBHI *turns the page, then looks at* JIMMIE.

The next page is a list written in green pen of the top-ten places to visit before you die.

JIMMIE. That's one of my mum's lists.

JIMMIE *is lost in her own thoughts.*

SUBHI. The Pyramids. Egypt. That's number one.

No reply from JIMMIE.

Maá used to tell me about my great-great-great-ba, from way back. He only had one foot, but he used to travel all over, healing everyone.

JIMMIE. Really?

SUBHI *nods.*

That's really cool.

SUBHI (*as if realising it for the first time*). It is, isn't it?

They both sit and think about their ancestors for a moment.

JIMMIE....Back when she was alive, and I couldn't sleep, Mum'd lie next to me and whisper these stories.

SUBHI. So there's more?

JIMMIE *nods.*

...Should I find the next bit? Keep reading?

JIMMIE *shakes her head.*

JIMMIE. I want to save them up. Make them last long, you know?

SUBHI *nods.* JIMMIE *gestures for the book.* SUBHI *carefully returns it under the fence, along with the torch.* JIMMIE *takes back the book, but gives* SUBHI *the feather.*

Thank you, Subhi.

Then JIMMIE *turns and leaves, disappearing into the shadows.*

DUCK. Wait till you hear my story. It's waaaaay better. Pirate Bill was once the fiercest duck pirate that ever roamed the seas –

SUBHI. Sssssh.

SUBHI shoves the DUCK in his pocket, lies down and puts his face on the earth again. He closes his eyes, still holding the feather.

Scene Seven

Day.

SUBHI *is sleeping on the ground, when members of the ensemble enter dressed as a group of rough BOYS.*

BOY ONE (*in Arabic*). There he is.

HEAD BOY (*in Arabic*). Get him.

The BOYS start kicking SUBHI on all sides. One grabs his face and holds his mouth closed. Another takes his shoes.

SUBHI wakes and tries to speak. He bites the hand on his face –

SUBHI. No! What are you doing? / Get off me! Get off me! What? What?

HEAD BOY (*in Arabic*). Where's the stash, kid? (*English.*) Where is it? Tell me!

SUBHI. Where is what?!

HEAD BOY. The packages. (*In Arabic.*) Where d'ya keep 'em?

Beat.

SUBHI (*lying*). Oh. I don't know. Eli knew all that.

The HEAD BOY *kneels down. He takes a long bit of wire out of his pocket.*

SUBHI. What are you –

HEAD BOY (*in Arabic*). Cut him.

The rest of the group hold him still, and one covers his mouth again, as the HEAD BOY *cuts* SUBHI *down his leg with his wire.*

We can't hear SUBHI *scream, but we can see that the pain is horrendous, and the shame unbearable.*

The HEAD BOY *motions to his* BOYS *to let go of* SUBHI.

SUBHI....In the back of the toilets, in Delta. There's some loose tiles. You can get across from Family through it.

HEAD BOY (*in Arabic*). It better be there.

SUBHI. It is.

One of the BOYS *takes out a rat caught in a trap. The* HEAD BOY *motions to it.*

HEAD BOY (*in Arabic*). Kill it.

SUBHI. What?

HEAD BOY (*in Arabic*). Kill it. And we won't bother you again.

SUBHI. What's wrong with you people –

HEAD BOY. Kill it, kid. Or you'll see us again tomorrow.

One of the BOYS *gives* SUBHI *the rat trap. He takes it, his hands shaking –*

And the day after that. (*In Arabic.*) And that. And that.

SUBHI, *crying now, slowly pushes down on the trap to kill the rat. The* BOYS *laugh.*

See ya, kid.

One of the BOYS *tries to take the feather too –*

BOY ONE (*in Arabic*). What is that?

SUBHI (*suddenly fierce*). NO!

BOY ONE (*in Arabic*). Weirdo.

They disappear.

SUBHI *sits, shaking, holding on to the feather. He looks at his leg; rolls his pants back down over the wound.*

Slowly, he rises and begins to limp back to the tent. He's sore, but okay.

SUBHI (*looking at the feather, holding it tightly*). So she is real.

HARVEY *and* BEAVER *are at the tent.*

MAÁ *is staring at them. She holds papers in her hands. She is motionless.*

BEAVER. We need you to confirm the identity –

HARVEY. Seriously?

BEAVER. How else are supposed to verify, Harvey?

BEAVER *shows* MAÁ *a photo. She takes it cautiously – looks and gasps, giving it back immediately.*

Yes?

MAÁ *nods.*

So that's a yes?

HARVEY. That's enough, Beaver. She said yes. C'mon. (*To* MAÁ.) I'm so sorry.

HARVEY *and* BEAVER *exit.*

MAÁ *stares in shock at the papers in her hands. Then she puts them under her pillow.*

Beat.

MAÁ *stands and rips down the blue fabric adorning her tent. She leaves it on the floor. Then she lies down in bed.*

SUBHI *arrives at the tent and immediately sees the fabric on the floor. He enters cautiously.*

SUBHI. Maá…? Maá?

MAÁ *stares straight ahead, unmoving.*

SUBHI *looks back the way he came. Then at* MAÁ *again.*

I just…

He goes in to hug his MAÁ. *Her body flinches. He steps back.*

I just need a –

MAA (*absolute*). No.

Beat.

SUBHI. Okay.

He sits down by her side. Tries a different tack – he sings/recites the verse from 'Lore Chandrani', mostly to settle himself down, to stop the shaking. MAÁ *grunts, and* SUBHI *pauses.*

An uncomfortable silence. Then:

MAÁ. No more.

SUBHI. What?

MAÁ. Looking back only brings sad, Subhi. Now look forward. No more back.

MAÁ *closes her eyes.*

SUBHI. Maá? Maá!

MAÁ *turns, away from the audience. She is absolutely still.*

Maá? Can you –

MAA (*suddenly enraged, screaming*). NO MORE!

SUBHI *is in shock – his mother has never spoken like that before.*

Beat.

MAÁ*'s body is unmoving.*

SUBHI *slowly backs away, then exits. He walks along the fence, thinking…*

NASIR (*offstage, calling out*). Subhi? Subhi?

NASIR *enters, stumbling along with his crutch, half-blind, coughing, shaking.*

(*Calling out.*) Subhi? Subhi? Subhi? / Subhi?

SUBHI. Nasir. Nasir! I'm here! What are you –

SUBHI *rushes over to him.*

NASIR. I wanted to tell you. Before, before, / before…

SUBHI. Before what?

NASIR (*concentrating*). I figured out what story to tell.

SUBHI. What?

NASIR. What I want you to draw for me.

SUBHI. Oh! Oh! That's great, Nasir. Why don't I walk you over to your tent, / and we'll –

NASIR. No no no no no / no no.

SUBHI. Um okay –

NASIR. Don't draw now. Not now. (*Concentrating.*) Later when you are free.

SUBHI.…You mean. When I get out?

NASIR *nods emphatically.*

I don't…

NASIR (*coughing, shaking*). Draw everything you saw in here. Draw that. When you get out. Draw that that / that that.

He nods again emphatically.

SUBHI. Okay. Okay, Nasir.

SUBHI*'s acceptance calms* NASIR *down.*

NASIR. I have present. For you.

He gives him a smooth black stone.

SUBHI. Um…

NASIR. Humour an old man man man. Hold it. Close your eyes.

SUBHI *does as he's told.*

Now think your happiest thought. Happy happy happy
happy –

SUBHI *thinks; animations appear. They suggest all sorts of
things:* BA *coming back, fruit salad, a donkey. But they
settle on that ghostlike image of* JIMMIE. SUBHI *smiles.*

Good. Open your eyes.

SUBHI *does.*

Now. Every time you hold your pebble, you remember your
think and smile.

Then NASIR *goes, mumbling, coughing, shaking.*

Good good good good good good good good good good –

SUBHI *walks.*

As he walks, QUEENY *and* ELI *enter from opposite ends
and meet on either side of the fence. They speak discreetly,
looking at an object that is hidden from us.* ELI *holds a set of
folded bedsheets in one arm.*

SUBHI *sees them and rushes towards them, excited to see*
ELI. QUEENY *shoves the item back into her pocket.*

SUBHI. Eli!

ELI. Little man!

They hold up their palms to touch from either side of the fence.

SUBHI. You... you seem okay?

ELI. Of course I'm okay, bud. I got this place worked out, don't
worry.

SUBHI *smiles, then his smile disappears, remembering*
MAÁ.

SUBHI. Queeny? / Maá is –

QUEENY. Go away, little brother.

SUBHI. But Maá –

QUEENY. Go away!

SUBHI *turns away, annoyed.*

ELI. Hey little man. Where's your shoes?

SUBHI turns and looks at ELI guiltily.

QUEENY. Subhi? Where's your shoes?

SUBHI's face crumbles.

SUBHI....I couldn't stop them, Eli. I tried... They were just too big.

ELI. Those boys? The big ones.

SUBHI nods.

QUEENY. What?!

SUBHI. They've been following me ever since you left –

QUEENY. Those bastards! I'm gonna rip them apart –

ELI. Leave it, Queeny. That'll just make things worse.

QUEENY (*to* SUBHI). Why didn't you tell me?

SUBHI gives QUEENY a look.

What?

SUBHI (*fierce*). As if you care.

This quietens QUEENY.

QUEENY. Did they hurt you?

Beat.

ELI. Did they hurt you, Subhi?

SUBHI....No, they didn't hurt me. But...

QUEENY. But what?

SUBHI....

ELI. What? It's okay, Subhi. Tell me.

SUBHI (*can't even look at* ELI). They made me tell 'em where the stash was.

ELI smiles.

ELI. Let 'em have it.

SUBHI. Huh?

ELI. The packages delivery business. Let 'em have it. It wouldn't have worked with me in here anyway, bud. I was tired of running it. And who needs shoes, hey? It's too hot.

None of them have shoes on. SUBHI *smiles.*

We'll just make do with stealing our own underwear and water and soap when we need it.

QUEENY. You shoulda come and told me, little brother.

Beat.

ELI. Show him, Queeny.

QUEENY....You sure?

ELI. Subhi won't tell.

QUEENY....I'm gonna show you something. But you can't tell anyone. You tell even that stupid duck you carry around and I swear, Subhi, I'll rub you in pig fat and set the Jackets' dogs on you, you hear?

The DUCK *squeaks in shock.*

SUBHI. I won't tell anyone. I promise.

Beat.

QUEENY *pulls out a camera.*

So that's what was in the package.

QUEENY. Obviously.

ELI. It's so people on the Outside know the truth. This camera, it sends the photos straight out into the world, right onto people's computers. We don't even have to plug it in. All we need is the WiFi.

SUBHI (*shocked*). But if you get caught –

ELI *laughs and shoves his hand through the fence, ruffling* SUBHI*'s hair.*

ELI. We won't get caught, little bruda. Don't you worry about that.

QUEENY *just shakes her head at her little brother.*

QUEENY. Some things are worth the risk, Subhi. Don't you see that? When are you ever going to notice what's going on around you? When are you going to grow up?

ELI. Leave it, Queeny. He's just a kid.

Another uncomfortable silence.

Subhi? Can I tell you something? Sometimes – sometimes, the sun is so burning hot that it sends these massive balls of fire straight at the earth. And the fire is so strong and hot that it could destroy the whole planet. But down here on earth, we're protected, right? By the atmosphere. So all we see are beautiful lights that dance across the sky. People come from all over just to see those lights dance. You can't see them from here, not ever, but someday, Subhi, you and me, we'll go to where you can see 'em, and we'll watch those lights boogie through the dark, yeah?

SUBHI (*smiling now*). While we're swimming, with the whale, and listening to the moon's secrets?

ELI. While we're swimming, with the whale, and drinking hot chocolate!

SUBHI. What?! Wow!

ELI. But for that day to come... (*Suddenly serious.*) we need to send out these pictures. You understand?

Beat.

SUBHI *nods.*

ELI *and* QUEENY *look around the camp to make sure none of the guards are around.*

ELI *looks to* QUEENY, *who prepares her camera, then nods.*

ELI *picks up the bedsheet and unfolds it. He puts it up against the fence so we can all see what is painted on it:*

'WE ARE INNOCENT.
PLEASE HELP US TO BE FREE.
WE CAN'T LIVE WITHOUT HOPE.'

For a moment, everything is still. ELI *looks around, and then whistles.*

The ensemble enter as REFUGEES *from the camp. They all lie down on the dirt.*

QUEENY *takes out the camera.*

SUBHI. No. No no / no no –

QUEENY. Ssssssh! Don't you get it, Subhi? They can do anything to us here, anything at all. That's why we're all dumped out here in the bum-end of nowhere. So everyone forgets us. Don't you see? Right now, we don't even exist. But that will change. We're gonna make the Outside remember us. Right, Eli?

ELI. Right.

QUEENY. I'm sick of being a dead rat, Subhi. Soon, the people out there will see us. They'll see that living in here isn't living at all. We just need to show them who we are, that we're people, and then they'll remember. Even if only a few people see, it will mean we're not invisible any more. D'you get it?

They stare at SUBHI. *Then he nods again, and stays quiet.*

I reckon this will make the newspaper.

ELI *whistles again, and they pose for* QUEENY. *She takes a photo. Another whistle, and everyone disperses as quietly as they entered.* ELI *hurriedly folds up the sheet and disappears too.*

SUBHI *is left alone, clutching his feather.*

End of Act One.

ACT TWO

Scene One

Night.

SUBHI*'s arm is shoved under the fence.* JIMMIE *is drawing a tattoo on it.*

JIMMIE. You can't look until it's finished, okay?

As she draws, the handcrafted animations appear again: feathers, fire…

I've got a joke for the duck. What do you call a duck who steals?

SUBHI. What?

JIMMIE. A robber duck.

They laugh.

DUCK. Mildly funny.

She finishes drawing. SUBHI *pulls his hand back in, looks.*

JIMMIE. It's meant to be a dragon but it kind of looks more like a duck. Sorry about that.

The DUCK *cheers.* SUBHI *looks at the dragon upside down.*

SUBHI. I think it looks like a dragon.

JIMMIE. It's meant to be like this dragon poster I have in my room. Maybe I should have practised first.

JIMMIE *passes* SUBHI *the pen under the fence, then shoves her arm through.*

Your turn. Make it good, coz it's permanent marker.

DUCK. Maybe she should have mentioned that before she drew her dragon-duck all over your arm.

SUBHI. Ssssh.

SUBHI *looks at* JIMMIE's *arm.*

Ouch.

JIMMIE. What?

SUBHI. That's a pretty bad scratch.

JIMMIE. Oh that? It's fine.

SUBHI. What happened?

JIMMIE. There's a nail sticking out from one of the drawers in my bedroom –

SUBHI. Oh! Did you show your dad?

JIMMIE. I'll show him on the weekend. Do you know what you wanna draw yet?

SUBHI....I think so.

> SUBHI *begins tattooing her arm. The animations untether, fly and re-transform.*

> (*As he draws.*) Jimmie?

JIMMIE. Yeah?

SUBHI....What's it like?

JIMMIE. What?

SUBHI. Your room.

JIMMIE. Like... a normal bedroom.

SUBHI. We live in a big tent. Our beds are made of steel. In those books Harvey brings me? None of the beds look like that.

> JIMMIE *stares at* SUBHI, *then nods, understanding.*

JIMMIE....Well, I have my bed in the corner, so when I'm lying on it I can look out the window to our back garden and the washing line. I have two pillows on my bed and a photo of my mum on the drawers next to it. I have the dragon poster and... my school bag. (*Shrugs.*) That's kind of it. And the walls are green.

> SUBHI *soaks up every word.*

SUBHI. When the people here tell me their stories, they're from far away. Stories from other countries and other times. Stories of getting here. But no one has a story from just Outside. None of us knows what it's like just the other side of the fences.

Beat.

JIMMIE. I'll show you all over someday, Subhi, I know this place better than anyone. Near my house there's this paperbark tree full of pink galahs. They always come before the rains. And there's an abandoned mine with the biggest holes I've ever seen in it. You could see them from space! And there's a lake in the desert! A real lake! I followed the birds there. Someday I'll take you everywhere there is to take and we'll explore together everything there is to explore. I promise, okay?

SUBHI....Okay.

SUBHI *nods, overwhelmed. He finishes the tattoo. The animations show Islamic calligraphy, in the shape of a small person.*

JIMMIE (*looking at it*). What is it?

SUBHI. It's the word for patience, in Arabic. In the shape of someone waiting by a river, for their best friend.

JIMMIE *looks at it for a long beat.*

JIMMIE. I love it. I'm going to take a photo and get it done as a real tattoo when I'm older.

SUBHI*'s smile is as wide as the sky.*

Thank you. (*Remembering something.*) Oh!

JIMMIE *gets a Thermos out of her bag and passes it under the fence to* SUBHI.

I brought some hot chocolate. Sorry. I know it's a stupid thing to drink when it's so hot but it's all I got.

SUBHI *just stares at it, gobsmacked.*

Go on. It's for you.

SUBHI. Is this real?

JIMMIE (*laughing*). What?

SUBHI. How did you manage to get hot chocolate?!

JIMMIE (*confused*). What…? Oh. Have you never had it before?

SUBHI. I didn't even know it existed until a few days ago.

JIMMIE. Well… I'm glad I get to be here for the first time you
try it.

JIMMIE *points at the Thermos.*

Go on.

SUBHI *opens the Thermos like it's a sacred gift. He drinks
slowly, but without stopping, for a long moment. Hot
chocolate runs over the corners of his mouth.*

(*Laughing.*) Guess you like it then?

SUBHI (*chocolate all over his face*)….All of life from now on
is meaningless.

JIMMIE *laughs some more.* SUBHI *drains more hot
chocolate. Before he realises it, it's all gone.*

Oh no. I'm so sorry –

JIMMIE. It's fine, I've got plenty more at home.

SUBHI. But you made it for us, and I had it all –

JIMMIE. Subhi! They're just little packets of powder you add
hot water to. I think Dad bought them like, / ten years or
something –

SUBHI. – no no no no no. I shouldn't have finished it. I should
have saved some. For Eli. When we get out of here we're
going to become world-famous hot-chocolate chefs –

JIMMIE. That sounds good. Can I join you?

SUBHI….Really?

JIMMIE (*shy*). I'll bring more next time, okay? For you to give
Eli.

SUBHI. Next time?

JIMMIE (*playing it cool*). Sure. Maybe even tomorrow night.

SUBHI (*smiling*)....That would be amazing.

JIMMIE *holds up the book.*

JIMMIE. Are you ready?

SUBHI *nods.* JIMMIE *passes it under the fence.* SUBHI *opens it, turns the pages –*

SUBHI. It was no surprise to anyone when Anka and Oto announced they were to be married.

Anka and Oto enter. Anka, now sixteen, is covered in henna and wears a bright, gorgeous scarf around her dress. Oto is dressed smartly too. It is their wedding dance. Anka has grown into a confident young woman; even though she is blind, she leads. She sings, and Oto follows where she goes.

Anka and Oto spent their days listening to the world in wonder. They listened to the trees sway with the wind, the ocean swell, birds fly over their heads.

In each other, they found peace.

And before too long, a child was on its way.

Anka's belly grows. She whispers to Oto – he listens at her belly. She is pregnant! They rejoice –

Mirka, older now, enters. She points to the horizon, alarmed.

Mirka was the first in the village to sense the danger that was coming. War. She could hear it on the wind.

There are distant sounds of war. But Anka and Oto smile and shake their heads, lost in the beauty of the natural world around them.

Oto and Anka were still young enough to find a new home. But why would they leave? They had everything they wanted, right here.

They wouldn't listen to Mirka.

Oto makes jokes to the baby in Anka's belly, and Anka laughs. Mirka turns to look at the horizon, filled with despair. There is a loud bomb blast –

JIMMIE. Subhi. (*Puts her hand up.*) Sorry.

SUBHI. Wait, just a bit more –

JIMMIE. Subhi. I don't want it to end. I want this to last.

Beat. SUBHI *nods and returns the book and torch –*

(*Pointing to the torch.*) No. Keep it.

She passes SUBHI *back the torch under the fence.*

We can use these to signal each other. Like Morse code or something.

DUCK. We are most definitely not allowed torches –

SUBHI *takes it.*

SUBHI. What's Morse code?

JIMMIE. Oh. Okay. Well, real Morse code uses a whole alphabet so you can write messages and everything. But we'll do our own one. I'll give three quick flashes on my torch to let you know I'm here, and you flash back three times if you're there and it's safe to come.

SUBHI *nods, with some skepticism.*

Two long flashes means help. That way, if ever you need me, you just flash, okay?

SUBHI. Got it. (*Does a discreet practice flash.*) But what if I need help when you're not at the fence?

JIMMIE. Oh yeah. Duh! Well, it might work further up the hill. I'll try, okay? Watch for me and flash back if you see me.

She turns to leave.

What do you see when a duck bends over?

DUCK (*offended*). Hey!

JIMMIE. Its bum quack.

She's gone. SUBHI*'s snorting with laughter.*

DUCK. That was mean.

SUBHI *walks back towards his tent.*

In the darkness, we see a flash of a torch. SUBHI *flashes back – quickly – then immediately hides the torch.*

JIMMIE *flashes three times.* SUBHI *returns them all.*

SUBHI *goes into his tent and lies down to sleep, smiling.*

Scene Two

Day.

QUEENY *wakes up* SUBHI.

QUEENY. You bloody well told, didn't you?

SUBHI *has no idea what* QUEENY *is talking about.*

DUCK. She's in a mood.

QUEENY *grabs* SUBHI*'s drawing.*

QUEENY. You told bloody Harvey, didn't you? You couldn't just keep your stupid big fat mouth shut, could you? And now everything is ruined!

DUCK. Never poke an angry duck. Best lesson I ever learnt, that.

SUBHI (*calmly*). I need that.

He gently takes the drawing back.

QUEENY. Yeah, well, we needed that camera, and now Harvey has it. Harvey said we were lucky it was him who found it because the other Jackets wouldn't just take it and forget. But I know it was you. At least what I'm doing is real –

SUBHI. This is real! It's not a story. It's a drawing for Jimmie. She's real. She's come in from Outside. You think you're so good, but Jimmie isn't scared of anything. She just walked right in here from the shadows, with a whole book of her Maá's –

QUEENY. Just shut up! Enough with your bloody stories!

She takes all of SUBHI*'s drawings and throws them everywhere. She rips the drawing of* JIMMIE *to shreds in a mad frenzy.*

SUBHI *turns to his mother, then back to* QUEENY.

SUBHI. I didn't tell Harvey about your stupid camera. I didn't tell anyone. I wouldn't do that to Eli. I wouldn't do that to you either.

Beat.

QUEENY. As if. Buttface.

QUEENY *spins around and leaves.* SUBHI *collects his drawings, seeing what he can recover.*

SUBHI. Jimmie is real, Maá. And she see can all the hidden bits, in all the corners of the universe... Maybe, when Ba finally arrives, and we go Outside to meet him, Jimmie can come with us too. She knows this place real well. She could probably take us all the way to the sea. What do you think?

HARVEY *enters, something on his mind. Then he sees* SUBHI*'s drawings on the floor.*

HARVEY. What happened here, Subhi?

SUBHI. Queeny thinks I told you about the camera.

HARVEY. Oh God. I'm sorry, bud. I can get more papers.

SUBHI. Thanks. And maybe some sticky tape too?

HARVEY. Yeah. And sticky tape too.

HARVEY *shifts, uncomfortable.*

SUBHI....Harvey?

HARVEY. I wanted to tell you. Before you heard it from someone else.

SUBHI. What?

HARVEY....We've lost another one, bud.

SUBHI. Who?

HARVEY. Nasir.

SUBHI. Oh. So that was why…

HARVEY. What?

SUBHI. Nothing.

SUBHI pulls out the stone, looks at it.

Another rat gone before they could break free.

HARVEY. C'mon, Subhi. He was old. You know that.

HARVEY gets close to SUBHI.

Listen. Tonight, you look up at that sky, and there will be a new star there. The brightest star in the sky. That will be Nasir.

SUBHI nods. HARVEY looks at MAÁ.

She still hasn't got up?

SUBHI. Not yet.

HARVEY. Hm.

Beat.

There's a new kid coming. To take Nasir's bed. I gotta go take him in. Just wanted to let you know. Personally.

SUBHI. Okay. Thanks, Harvey.

HARVEY leaves.

As SUBHI picks up his drawings, he sings what he can remember of 'Lore Chandrani'.

The sound of rain grows.

Feathers fall from the sky. BA's whispers grow.

Day becomes night. The Night Sea is wild.

Scene Three

The spot.

SUBHI *looks up at the sky.*

SUBHI….Harvey reckons that when someone dies, they turn into a star.

   JIMMIE *looks up at a bright star.*

JIMMIE. Well, if he's right, that star there looks like a pretty good one.

   SUBHI *sees it, and nods.*

SUBHI. Hello, Nasir.

   Beat.

   Better up there than in here, I suppose.

JIMMIE. Maybe that one is my mum, and they're hanging out now.

SUBHI. They'd just tell stories to each other forever.

   SUBHI *is smiling, a little bit.*

JIMMIE. Hey. Look what I brought!

   JIMMIE *pulls a poor man's feast out of her bag.*

   (*Pulling out two Chupa Chups.*) Entrée. Found these down the back of the couch.

   She passes one to SUBHI *through a whole in the fence.*

SUBHI. What are they?

JIMMIE. Sweet sweet sugar on a stick.

SUBHI (*tasting it*). Incredible.

JIMMIE (*pulling out a packet of Twisties*). Main meal. Cheesy, puffy goodness.

SUBHI. / Mmmmmmm…

She pulls out and shakes her Thermos.

JIMMIE. And dessert.

SUBHI. More hot chocolate?!

JIMMIE. Yep!

SUBHI. Eek! (*Shifts.*) But… Would you mind if I kept these, and shared them later, with Maá and Queeny and Eli? Maá's been sleeping a lot lately. Maybe this would… wake her up, you know?

JIMMIE. Why don't we share my part, and you keep those for your family?

SUBHI. Thank you.

JIMMIE *passes some Twisties under the fence.* SUBHI *sees her arm again –*

Jimmie!

JIMMIE. What?

SUBHI. Your scratch.

JIMMIE. Oh that?

SUBHI. It's gotten worse!

JIMMIE. It's fine!

SUBHI. Seriously. Did you show it to your dad?

JIMMIE. He'll be back home tonight. I'll show it to him then.

SUBHI. Promise?

JIMMIE. God, you remind me of my mum!

She eats some Twisties.

(*Motioning to* SUBHI.) Go on!

SUBHI (*eating them*). This. Is. Amazing.

They laugh. Over the course of the scene, they share their feast.

JIMMIE. So what did you do today? Anything fun?

SUBHI....I worked out that about one-third of our time awake is spent standing in lines. And today that would have been longer because just when I got to the front of the line at breakfast, the Jacket saw I'd forgotten my ID card, so I had to get it and line up again.

JIMMIE....Okay.

SUBHI. I also drew something for you. But Queeny ripped it up.

JIMMIE. What a buttface.

SUBHI *laughs*.

SUBHI. She didn't used to be like that. Queeny.

JIMMIE. Yeah?

SUBHI. She used to talk about Someday. The day we'd get out of here. She used to...

JIMMIE (*soft*). Tell me.

SUBHI. Queeny would make things for me. Little people from rope and sticks. I'd sort through the stick people and choose one to be our *Ba*. Queeny would say 'ói!' and her head would nod yes. 'That's our Ba!' Then all of us Stick People would walk out of those fences, like the only reason every one of us was in here was to wait for my Ba to come...

JIMMIE. And one day he will.

SUBHI *nods*.

SUBHI....That was back when Queeny was still good at playing. Back then, Queeny would pretend she was a baddy and chase me over the dirt and catch me and tickle me until the breath got too tight in my chest and I'd snort out snot. Queeny taught me about all sorts. About how to swim and how to ride a donkey and how to climb trees. And even though there was no river or donkey or trees, she'd still make me practise, imagining as best we could. Her favourite was the tree climbing. She told me all about the tree she used to climb back in Burma, and how you just have to take it one step at a time and not look down until you reach the last branch. Then when you do, you can breathe in the brand-new air that is sweet and fresh from the clouds and the best air in the whole world to breathe... Now Queeny doesn't want to play any more. And she never talks about the Someday. When we'll get out.

JIMMIE....So you have climbed a tree before. In your head anyway.

SUBHI. I never got it until now. That we aren't wanted in this place, or in Burma, or in any other place. I didn't get that we aren't wanted anywhere. For a long time I thought we were just waiting on my Ba, is all.

JIMMIE....I've got something to show you, Subhi.

She pulls out a phone, shows it to SUBHI.

My dad's old phone. Sorry, there's no credit. In case you wanted to call anyone.

SUBHI *gestures at the sky.*

SUBHI. I don't have his number.

They smile a little more. JIMMIE *leans in close and presses buttons on the phone. The images appear where we've been seeing the animations.*

JIMMIE. That's –

SUBHI. That's Raticus. Duh.

JIMMIE. Yep.

SUBHI. You're right. He does look smart.

JIMMIE (*proud*). Thank you.

The photo is of Raticus inside an old cardboard box. The box is on a crappy chest of drawers that is falling apart. The next photo is a sad but gentle man.

SUBHI. That's your dad, isn't it?

JIMMIE *nods. The man sits in the kitchen of a ramshackle house. Only cheap, processed foods can be seen. The man is tired and overweight. She goes to the next photo – a tidy, beautiful patch of plants amidst an otherwise mess of a frontyard.*

Wow.

JIMMIE. That's Dad's garden.

SUBHI. It's beautiful.

JIMMIE. Like I said. He's good with his hands.

SUBHI. What's that?

JIMMIE. A bird bath.

SUBHI. A what?

JIMMIE. A place for birds to come and sit and drink before they
fly on to… wherever they were going.

SUBHI. Oh.

JIMMIE. This is a lemon tree. And that bathtub with dirt in it is
a place to grow veggies.

SUBHI. Weird.

JIMMIE. It's not weird. When Mum was alive she used to go
out in the garden on Sunday morning and make pancakes
with lemon and sugar and get veggies from the bathtub and it
was great, okay?

SUBHI. Okay. Sorry.

Beat.

Maybe you could grow veggies again.

JIMMIE. Dad and I aren't doing that any more. Mum needs to
be there.

SUBHI. The birds would be with you instead.

JIMMIE.…Maybe.

JIMMIE *clicks the phone. The next photo is of the Outside –
a lagoon.*

SUBHI. Whoa. Is that the lake in the desert?!

JIMMIE (*nodding*). I'll take you here.

SUBHI. That's real?

JIMMIE. It's basically just down the road!

SUBHI *looks past the razor-wire fence.* JIMMIE *presses more buttons – there's a flurry of pictures of trees and tracks and lakes and rocks –*

I'll take you here too, and here and here and here and here and here and maybe we'll even grow veggies together with the birds!

SUBHI *giggles at the thought, until they're both laughing loudly.*

SUBHI. Ssssssh!

JIMMIE *pulls* SUBHI *in for a selfie.*

JIMMIE. Don't look at me – look at the phone, duh. And smile, Subhi!

She takes the photo and shows it to SUBHI. *He looks at it wonder, lost in it, until* JIMMIE *shows him the book:*

Just a little bit? Please?

She passes the book to SUBHI. SUBHI *looks up at the bright star, then reads.*

SUBHI. The soldiers came at night.

Soldiers stride in.

Elsewhere, Anka and Oto hide in a corner.

Anka and Oto wished that they'd heeded Mirka's warnings. They waited and hoped and prayed that they wouldn't be found.

But no one could hide from the soldiers.

The soldiers find Anka and Oto, who resist capture. There is a struggle – Oto is knocked out, Anka is taken. The soldiers exit with her. Oto's body remains on the stage.

Mirka enters, hands wrapped around the Bone Sparrow.

All night Mirka had held the Bone Sparrow, pulling in its protection. She had watched the events unfold, fully aware she couldn't help a single soul.

She found Oto in the morning.

Mirka goes to Oto, fearing the worst. She helps him revive.

He was still breathing.

When Oto realises Anka is gone, he howls.

Mirka knew then that it was Oto who needed the Bone Sparrow most of all.

Mirka places the necklace around Oto's neck.

Mirka told Oto that the Sparrow would recognise Anka's soul. It would lead him to her.

So Oto left; walking the long road to the top of the mountain and away from home, holding the Bone Sparrow tightly all the way.

Suddenly, JIMMIE *takes her Bone Sparrow off, shoves it under the fence and wraps* SUBHI*'s hands around it.*

JIMMIE. Can you feel it? That's what she's doing. She's keeping the clan safe. That means you too, Subhi.

They sit there like that, SUBHI *in shock at the closeness,* JIMMIE *in need of someone to know.*

SUBHI....I hope so.

As SUBHI *turns the page, Mirka and Oto disappear.* JIMMIE *loosens her hand from* SUBHI*'s, peels herself and the Bone Sparrow away –*

There's... some directions on how to get to Eva's house.

JIMMIE....I didn't know that bit. Maybe I've just forgotten, but I'd know, wouldn't I? If I'd heard this before?

SUBHI....Maybe. Maybe she got distracted in the telling? Or maybe you were just too little.

JIMMIE. But what if it's not that? What if I'm forgetting? Sometimes... Sometimes when I close my eyes, I can't even remember what Mum looks like. You know? Not really.

SUBHI *takes her hand this time, and they look up at the stars.*

SUBHI. It doesn't matter what you see. I think it just matters what you feel.

JIMMIE *nods, then stares at* SUBHI *for a long moment.*

What?

JIMMIE *pulls a pair of wire cutters from her bag.*

JIMMIE. I've gotta go... Come with me?

SUBHI....Whoa.

JIMMIE. If we cut all night, we'd make a hole big enough to fit you through I reckon.

She's serious.

Pause.

The duck could come too.

SUBHI *takes a long look back to where his family are sleeping in their tent.*

Then he shakes his head.

SUBHI. My Maá...

JIMMIE *nods.*

JIMMIE. Take them, then. In case you change your mind.

She passes the cutters underneath the fence.

And once you're out? You head straight towards that old gum almost at the top of the hill. When you reach that, you'll see my house further on. It's the only house with a letter box made out of Lego.

SUBHI....Okay.

JIMMIE. Are you sure you don't want to come with me?

Another pause. But SUBHI *stays put.* JIMMIE *lets the cutters go.*

Okay. See ya.

SUBHI. See ya.

Then she's gone.

SUBHI *sits in the dark, next to the fence. He stares at the cutters.*

DUCK. Leave it.

SUBHI. What would you know? You're just a stupid duck.

DUCK. What would you know? You're just a stupid boy. In some countries in the world, ducks are kings, you know.

SUBHI. The stuff of kings…

SUBHI picks the cutters up.

Beat.

SUBHI takes off his shirt and wraps the cutters inside. Then he exits, slowly.

DUCK. Why does no one listen to me?

Scene Four

Day.

SUBHI *and* QUEENY *wait near* MAÁ*'s side as a* DOCTOR *prods and pokes her.*

HARVEY *and* BEAVER *watch from a distance.*

MAÁ *breathes evenly but otherwise makes no response to the* DOCTOR*'s prodding.*

The DOCTOR *finishes his brief checks, and motions to* HARVEY *and* BEAVER *as he leaves. The men all exit for a moment.*

SUBHI. Do you think if we gave her some Twisties –

QUEENY. Shut up.

They wait in silence.

HARVEY *comes back alone.*

HARVEY. Queeny.

She turns to HARVEY*, already knowing what he's going to say.*

The doc says we gotta put Maá on HRAT watch.

SUBHI. Why would you do that?

QUEENY. Quiet, Subhi!

HARVEY. This might need to be a convo between me and your big sister, / mate.

SUBHI. But the watch is for people who try to hurt themselves into dying. / Maá's not –

QUEENY. Why don't you listen to me when I tell you to shut up!

SUBHI. Maybe it's a snake bite, / making Maá sleep like that –

QUEENY. For God's sake, just STOP TALKING!

Beat.

SUBHI. Maá's just tired. That's all.

Beat.

HARVEY. Don't worry, bud. We just need to check on her more often because she hasn't eaten much or had much to drink for a while and we just want to make sure she is okay. It's good that we'll be checking in on your Maá more regularly.

HARVEY *exits.*

SUBHI. She'll wake up soon. When she's ready.

QUEENY. Don't you understand anything, Subhi? Coming here is like waking up from a nightmare and then finding out that you aren't awake at all. Maá's the one who's being sensible. We're the idiots, pretending like everything's normal. Sometimes I wonder if you even –

SUBHI. I get it.

QUEENY. What?

SUBHI. I get it. Maá's eyes are shut so she doesn't have to see everything any more.

QUEENY (*quietened*).... Yeah. That's right, Subhi. That's right.

SUBHI *stares at his* MAÁ.

There are sounds outside – ELI*'s voice.* SUBHI *and* QUEENY *leave the tent to go to him.*

ELI *holds a folded bedsheet and paces angrily by the fence, shouting in his mother tongue:*

ELI (*repeating*). How are we supposed to live?

SUBHI *rushes to him.*

SUBHI. Eli? / Eli! Eli –

ELI. We told them we're not going back. We can do that, the lawyers told us. We can refuse to go back. But they still came up with a way to hurt us. They're sending us away, / and –

SUBHI. What, when?

ELI. Next week –

QUEENY. No! No no no no no –

As the action below unfolds, QUEENY *starts pacing up and down, repeating and talking to herself.*

ELI. They say they're moving a whole lot of us from Alpha. They reckon it's getting too full in here, so we have to go to a Transit Centre. In another country, Subhi. A country whose people don't want us. They did it before – they put people into the Transit Centre and they all got beaten up and pissed on and the police were there and didn't even try to stop it. They joined in! We can go Outside there, but we can't work, or go to school, or anything. We won't even have enough money to buy food. How are we supposed to live? How are we...

He breaks down. SUBHI *has never seen him like this, and doesn't know what to do.*

I'm scared, Subhi. I don't want to go. I'm not a grown-up. I don't want to be one yet.

SUBHI *squashes his head against the fence, against* ELI.

SUBHI. Eli? Eli. There's a girl –

ELI. Subhi? What are you talking about?

SUBHI. There's a girl. She can help. She could look after you, or, or –

ELI. What girl?

SUBHI. Maybe she could help you get out –

ELI. And go where? Hiding from the police the whole time? You and Queeny and your Maá – you're my family, you understand? You're the only ones I have left / in the entire –

SUBHI. I know but still. / Eli, you said next week!

ELI. Subhi? Subhi!… Did you really meet someone? From the Outside?

SUBHI *looks around, and then nods.*

SUBHI. She even has hot chocolate, Eli. And she knows the way to the ocean! She could take you, / to the whale, to hear the moon's secrets –

ELI. Good. That's really good, Subhi. Now listen to me. Are you listening?

SUBHI. Yes.

ELI. The time might come when you need to get away. Do you understand?

SUBHI. This isn't for me, it's for you –

ELI. Subhi! Listen to me! This country won't have us. Not ever. Not. Ever. Do you understand? Are you listening to me?

SUBHI. But –

ELI. So you keep talking to that girl, and you use her if you need to, okay?

SUBHI. But they're sending you away – You need to –

QUEENY. No.

They turn to QUEENY.

We have a different plan. Don't we, Eli?

ELI. Queeny –

QUEENY. We have to do it, Eli!

SUBHI. Do what?

QUEENY. We have to do it. Before you or Maá... (*Can't finish the sentence*.) Before more of us go. Without knowing the Outside.

Pause.

Then ELI *nods.*

ELI (*to* QUEENY). Okay.

QUEENY. Okay.

ELI. I'll organise this side. You do yours?

QUEENY *nods too.*

Okay.

SUBHI *stares at them both.*

SUBHI. Eli? Queeny?

ELI (*ignoring* SUBHI). When?

QUEENY. We've been preparing for this for some time, Eli.

ELI. Yeah. I know... Tonight?

QUEENY *nods.*

QUEENY. Tonight.

SUBHI. Guys?

QUEENY *and* ELI *exit in different directions, leaving* SUBHI *on his own again.*

Scene Five

Night. It's filthy hot.

Low drumming.

SUBHI *stands still and watches as:*

– On the inside, people are holding up signs and chanting. Some of them have their lips sewn together. They are a dishevelled, disheartened lot, but in their protest, they still have their dignity.

– On the outside, a handful of protestors are chanting too, joining in on the protest.

– QUEENY and ELI, caked in sweat, set fire to two different parts of the stage. This act is done with reverence, urgency and rage. They are fed up. This is their protest.

Over the course of the scene, the smoke grows and takes over the stage.

HARVEY *enters.* (SUBHI *observes this conversation, shocked.*)

HARVEY (*to* QUEENY). What the hell do you think you're doing?

QUEENY. What else could we do?

HARVEY. You think this will help, Queeny? You think this will somehow make things better? Here I am, trying to do / everything I can to –

ELI (*from the other side of the stage*). NO MORE!

QUEENY. C'mon, Harvey. Stop kidding yourself. You know what you are. What we are.

HARVEY. What are you?

QUEENY. We're the dead rats they leave out to stop other rats from coming, Harvey. 'Cept these rats aren't gonna stay dead, you understand?

HARVEY. Queeny –

ELI (*from the other side of the stage*). NO MORE!

HARVEY. Eli –

QUEENY *and* ELI. NO MORE!

They continue yelling as smoke overtakes the stage. We can't really see anyone, just shapes. QUEENY *and* ELI's *voices are moving; they're not still. As* HARVEY *exits, we hear his voice in the mix too:*

HARVEY (*into walkie-talkie*). Back-up. We need back-up. Immediately. Do you hear me? Now!

SUBHI is the only one we can really see. He backs away in fear, and walks around the camp, calling out:

SUBHI. Queeny! Queeny!

But there is no response from his sister. The protest continues, and goes into a riot.

SUBHI is walking along the fence and arrives at the spot when he suddenly sees JIMMIE, *waiting there.*

Jimmie?!

JIMMIE (*as if playing a macabre game*). Found you.

She looks… weird. Weak. Disorientated. She holds her arm, where the wound has got infected.

SUBHI. What are you doing here?

JIMMIE. I need…

SUBHI. What?

JIMMIE. Sorry. I just – I didn't know where else to…

She slumps onto the dirt. Her body is limp. SUBHI *rushes to her; but she's on the other side of the fence.*

SUBHI. Jimmie!

JIMMIE *closes her eyes, and waits.*

SUBHI *stares at her, helpless.*

JIMMIE *opens her eyes and looks at* SUBHI.

JIMMIE. Well, come on then. Don't you know how to read?

SUBHI. Read?

JIMMIE (*looks down at* SUBHI*'s lap, points to the book she thinks is there*). Read.

SUBHI *shows his empty hands.*

Oh.

JIMMIE *grapples with her backpack; takes it off, opens it. Her mum's book tumbles out –*

SUBHI. Jimmie –

JIMMIE (*distant, talking to herself*). You know. I saw. The photo. In the paper.

SUBHI....So Queeny was right.

Beat.

(*Pointing at it.*) Jimmie. The book.

JIMMIE. Those crocodiles wouldn't bother with me. I'm too small. I'll be okay.

SUBHI. What?

JIMMIE. In the lagoon.

JIMMIE *begins to crawl across the red earth, stumbling away through the smoke.*

SUBHI. Jimmie!

She's gone.

SUBHI *stares at the book.*

She'll come back for it.

He waits.

She'll come back for it.

She hasn't.

Then, out of the smoke, two long flashes.

SUBHI *sees.*

Pause.

Then SUBHI *turns and runs back through the escalating riot, to a secret part of the stage.*

Come on come on come on –

He uncovers the wire cutters and the food from JIMMIE. *He takes the wire cutters. Then runs back to the spot.*

Madly, he cuts away at the bottom of the fence and digs at the dirt until there is enough room for him to crawl underneath.

Elsewhere onstage, the sound of the riots grows and grows. There are more scuffles.

As SUBHI *is digging, he comes upon an object that shocks him.*

He pauses.

Then lifts up a sheathed knife.

SUBHI *turns back to look at the chaos erupting across the centre – and decides to keep the knife. He puts it in his pocket.*

He crawls underneath the fence – the fence cuts into his back but he manages to sneak through – and picks up the book.

Then he runs the way JIMMIE *told him to; runs to her house.*

As he runs, the riots break open the set. Scuffles with DETAINEES *break down fences. The stage becomes a mess.*

SUBHI *finds* JIMMIE *collapsed on the ground, right under a letter box made of Lego.*

SUBHI *checks* JIMMIE *the same way the* DOCTOR *checked his* MAÁ; *her rolls her into the recovery position.*

In one hand JIMMIE *clenches a torch, in the other she clenches that phone.*

SUBHI *pries the phone out of* JIMMIE's *hand, presses buttons madly, then stares at the screen:*

Emergency only. Zero zero zero.

He dials '0-0-0'.

PHONE. You have dialled emergency triple-zero. Your call is being connected... please wait.

JIMMIE *groans*.

SUBHI. Hold on, Jimmie. Hold on.

PHONE. Police, fire or ambulance?

SUBHI....Ambulance?

SUBHI *waits. The sounds of the riots continue – they are just more far off now.*

PHONE. Ambulance Emergency, what is your exact location?

SUBHI. I don't know... I need an ambulance. Jimmie is sick and hot and isn't breathing right and I don't know the address or anything, but there isn't... it's near the house up the hill from the detention centre. You go straight up the hill and head for the big gum and then you'll see the house with a Lego letter box and a bath in the garden and a tree and you come out the back of that and you'll finds us on the dirt. Dirt I've never walked on before. A world I've never seen bef–

PHONE. It's okay, son. We have the address of that house and an ambulance is on the way. Is she conscious? Is she breathing? I need you to roll her on to her side and keep her calm. Keep her awake. You're pretty far away from us, okay? Keep her awake. Can you do that, son?

JIMMIE *suddenly grabs* SUBHI*'s arm.*

JIMMIE. Subhi. Subhi?

SUBHI. Eeek!

PHONE. Son?

JIMMIE. A story...

SUBHI *drops the phone and takes* JIMMIE*'s hand and wraps it around the Bone Sparrow, holding his hand over hers.*

He opens the book to where they last left off –

SUBHI. C'mon. Quirkiest phone numbers. Top-ten favourite chocolates. How to make egg-free banana bread in five minutes. C'mon! Oh –

(*Reading*.) Wherever the soldiers went, Anka went too.

Anka enters and walks – flanked by soldiers, a baby strapped to her back.

She was able to do something the soldiers could not: cook. Her newborn baby was always kept close, strapped to her body.

Oto enters and walks – and walks and walks.

Oto walked the long road, past the mountains and all the way to the sea. He began to wonder if he would ever see Anka again.

The soldiers halt.

Eventually, the soldiers stopped fighting. They could bear it no longer. Anka's presence only reminded them of their own families. But before they deserted their generals, they made sure to get Anka a place on a boat heading to a foreign land.

Anka boards a boat.

Anka knew she would never set foot on her homeland again.

Oto boards a boat.

War had devastated Oto's country. He had worked countless jobs just to survive. He realised he would never see his wife again, or meet his child. It was time to leave.

The boat leaves the shore.

As the boat left the shore, he felt the hope that had carried him this far vanish into a pit of dread.

A baby's cry. Anka sings –

And then –

Oto hears the baby's cry; he hears Anka's song. He walks towards them.

They embrace.

Oto kisses his wife and son many, many times. He takes the Bone Sparrow from around his neck puts it on his son.

May you forever bring us luck and protection and may you carry our souls to freedom.

SUBHI *closes the book. But Oto and Anka's song of reunion can still be heard.*

There is an ending.

The sirens of an ambulance. SUBHI *jumps up with a start: he can't be seen here. He rises, and rushes back to the camp.*

As JIMMIE*'s body is carried off, the camp's chaos overtakes the stage. Her body is one amongst others.*

As he passes the trees, SUBHI *pauses at them –*

(*As he climbs.*) Don't look down. Don't look down. (*Repeats.*)

From the top of the tree, SUBHI *can see the chaos.* HARVEY *and* BEAVER *– dressed in riot gear now – have managed to gather and put away everyone – herding them all onto one part of the stage, clumped together.*

But not ELI.

ELI *avoids capture, and as he runs,* BEAVER *chases him, becoming increasingly furious.*

ELI *runs to the spot. He falls over, and scrambles, digging at the ground furiously. Looking for something.*

Looking for a knife that is no longer there.

When he realises that it's not there, and the fence has been partly cut apart by someone, he tries to crawl underneath, almost escaping –

But BEAVER *drags him back by the legs and spins him around.*

No!

SUBHI *scrambles down the tree and runs to them –*

BEAVER *drops his riot shield and begins to hit* ELI *with his stick, again and again. He shouts in between the hits:*

BEAVER. You bastards – Think you're doing something – All your trouble is doing – is making it worse for everyone – If you had only been quiet and waited and obeyed it would all be fine. It's all your fault. Your fault. Your fault –

SUBHI *arrives at the scene. He takes out the knife –*

ELI *sees him, and doesn't say anything, but wills* SUBHI *to use the weapon on* BEAVER *with his eyes, his body –*

BEAVER *strikes* ELI *again –*

SUBHI *can't. He can't do it. He drops the knife and slinks away, and watches from the corner as* BEAVER *beats* ELI *to near-death.*

HARVEY *arrives, furious. He rushes to* ELI *and feels for a pulse.* BEAVER *backs away.*

HARVEY*'s entrance jerks* SUBHI *out of his shock. He suddenly remembers what else is in his pocket.* JIMMIE*'s phone. He pulls it out, and starts recording.*

HARVEY (*to* BEAVER). What did you do?! (*To* ELI, *shaking him.*) C'mon, kid. C'mon!

HARVEY *grabs his walkie-talkie:*

At the perimeter fence. South side. Near those tall gum trees. We need the doctor here. Now!

There's no answer.

We need to go get help. C'mon. C'mon!

HARVEY *grabs* BEAVER, *pulling him to go, when* ELI*'s body twitches. His hands move. He slowly rises to his feet, grinning madly –*

ELI. Wait till the world sees this. What you've done to us. What you do to us –

SUBHI *watches as* BEAVER *pushes* HARVEY *off him, raises his stick in the air, and hits* ELI *one more time.*

ELI *falls. His body doesn't move any more.*

HARVEY *is frozen, looking at* ELI.

BEAVER *sees the dropped knife on the ground. He picks it up, thinking. He nods.*

Then BEAVER *exits, pushing past* HARVEY. *The act spins* HARVEY *around, and he sees* SUBHI.

SUBHI *and* HARVEY *stare at each other for a moment.*

Then HARVEY *rushes after* BEAVER, *exiting.*

SUBHI *crawls over to* ELI, *in shock. Checks his body like the* DOCTOR *checked his mum's.*

But there's no helping this one.

SUBHI *grieves.*

He lies down next to ELI, *with his ear to the earth.*

We are like this for a long moment, as smoke billows across the stage and the fires settle into ash.

HARVEY *returns in a rush, alone –*

HARVEY. What happened, Subhi? Did you see? Tell me, Subhi. What did you see? What did you see, kid?

SUBHI *looks at* HARVEY *like he knows, but he doesn't say anything.* HARVEY *shakes* SUBHI –

What did you see?!

– then relents, releasing him. HARVEY *collapses.*

I tried. I tried, okay?

SUBHI *doesn't say anything. He just looks at* HARVEY. HARVEY *leaves.*

SUBHI *slowly gets up, and walks.*

A DOCTOR *finds him, and gives him water.* QUEENY *is close behind –*

QUEENY. Subhi!

QUEENY *hugs her brother tight.*

SUBHI. Maá! Where's Maá? Where's –

QUEENY. She's alright, Subhi. Don't worry. She's alright.

QUEENY*'s head is cut, and the* DOCTOR *goes to her –*

DOCTOR. We need to have a look at that –

QUEENY. No. My brother.

He checks SUBHI.

DOCTOR. He's fine. (*To* QUEENY.) You, on the other hand –

The DOCTOR *takes* QUEENY *and leaves* SUBHI *reeling, alone onstage.*

Scene Six

MAÁ, *in her tent, alone. But she is not sleeping. She is putting the blue fabric back up.*

The task complete, she sits upright on her bed and waits. She has a book on her lap.

QUEENY, *her head bandaged, enters with* SUBHI.

MAÁ *pulls* SUBHI *into her arms. Then she puts him down, and gives him the book.*

She speaks in a mixture of English and Ruáingga.

MAÁ. It's Ba's. It's your father's poems.

SUBHI *takes the book, begins to look through it.*

SUBHI. It's mostly in *Ruáingga*.

MAÁ. I will teach you.

QUEENY *smiles*.

QUEENY.…That girl. The one you were making the pictures for. She's real, isn't she?

SUBHI *nods*.

I'm sorry, Subhi. I should've listened.

SUBHI. I hope you can meet her one day, Queeny.

QUEENY. Someday.

SUBHI *smiles*.

QUEENY *goes and sits by her mother. They share a look, then both look at* SUBHI *for a long moment*.

MAÁ *takes* SUBHI*'s hand*.

MAÁ. Subhi…? Ba is dead. He's been killed. I know it's true because I saw. They showed me photos. After that I… It was like the light had been pulled out of the world. What had we come all this way for, then, for him not to follow?

QUEENY. I'm sorry, Subhi. But Maá… Maá wanted to tell you herself. She kept saying she would, that she just wanted to find the right time. And then she started sleeping more and…

Long pause.

SUBHI (*despondent*). So I'll never meet him.

MAÁ. It doesn't matter that you didn't meet him. You are so much like him.

BA *enters, and watches his family*.

SUBHI. I'm not like him. Ba was brave, and spoke the truth. Ba would have stopped Beaver. I just…

MAÁ. You are just a boy. You are like your Ba, but you have not become him yet. Someday, though…

As MAÁ *speaks,* SUBHI *stands and walks to the ghost of his father, staring at him, studying him*.

QUEENY. Someday, you will become him.

As MAÁ *speaks,* SUBHI *turns to her, taking in what she says*.

MAÁ. And you will tell our story. Of not being allowed… Of how we woke up one day to find we were no longer citizens in our own country. Of Queeny not being allowed to go to school or Ba to work or me to the hospital. Of having our house burnt down, and our animals killed. Of being arrested.

Of the military taking away our rights, our food, our property, our access to any land. Of running from the police and soldiers. So much running... Of Ba being arrested for writing his poems, and not being allowed to come back. Of our friends disappearing and people dying. Of being attacked by the military, again, and again, and again, until we got the message. You are not welcome here and you will never be welcome here. Of fleeing. A million people on a thousand boats. Fleeing. Not to one place, but many. A breaking up that can never be put together again. Of every new land telling us that we don't belong. Not in their place. Not in any place. So now – an endless waiting. Of becoming the largest group of people in the world with nowhere to live. And knowing that if we go back home, to Burma, we'd be killed. We would be returning to a genocide. But we do belong, Subhan. We made it here. And we are here. We survived a genocide. And so now, we do belong.

SUBHI *can only stare at his mother.*

Someday, you will tell our stories. You will say: we exist. Just like Ba.

SUBHI (*turning back to his father*). Someday?

BA *reaches his hand out, and* SUBHI *reaches his out to touch him.*

BA *nods, and* SUBHI *nods too.*

(*Turning back to his mother.*) Okay. If you teach me.

MAÁ. I will.

MAÁ *holds up the book of poems.*

On the very last page, there's a poem dedicated to you.

Simultaneously, BA *recites the poem in Ruáingga and* SUBHI *reads the English translation from the book. It is the same poem* BA *recited in the opening scene of the play.*

BA (*reciting a poem in Ruáingga*) Zindigi dase ekkan-ziyol

SUBHI. Life is an open prison

BA. Ara asman arde-tara okkol-dekifarir

SUBHI. We can see the sky and stars

BA. Ara tanda-mesus gorir

SUBHI. We can feel the breeze

BA. Lekin ara honodin uri-zai-nofarir

SUBHI. But we can never fly away

BA. Asman dase arar seema

SUBHI. The sky is the limit

BA. Ara merid oileeo

SUBHI. yet we are the ground

BA. Lekin ai aicho arar arkanor hawa-loi-farir, zendila miuewla-okkol fazi aiyeer

SUBHI. But I can still breathe the air of my motherland as it sweeps through the clouds

BA *and* MAÁ. Ekidin ara fak okkol banai-fajum ar-enor-uray sori faijum

SUBHI. One day we will grow wings and ride upon it.

BA, *content now, exits.*

SUBHI *looks up. There is rain. Real rain.*

MAÁ. Is that… rain?

MAÁ *and* QUEENY *turn to it.*

QUEENY. It… It is!

They run out, and stand underneath it.

MAÁ. Long time back, there was no rain. In the old country. Many years, no rain. Then your Ba was born, Subhan, and that rain fell from the sky. Just like this. Since you were born it was waiting to flood on your head. Just like the whole country is waiting. For you.

HARVEY *enters.*

HARVEY. It's done.

MAÁ. Come, my son.

SUBHI *looks for his torch, and finds it.*

SUBHI. Just in case.

HARVEY. Where'd you get that?

SUBHI. My friend. Jimmie.

SUBHI *exits, and they follow. They see a tall ladder*
HARVEY*'s put up next to a ledge. They walk to it, all four of*
them. It's near where the weak spot used to be, where SUBHI
used to meet JIMMIE.

They climb the ladder, and sit on the ledge. QUEENY
gestures past the trees, past everything –

QUEENY. Do you see, brother? Right on the horizon. It's the
sea.

The sound of the sea rises and fills the room.

SUBHI....So that's what it looks like.

MAÁ....Someday, you will feel it too. Someday, we will all
feel it again.

They sit and watch the sea, which fills the animations in
waves of colour.

SUBHI *watches the sea, and hears the call of a whale. In the*
animations, the whale's song pulls the moon down to the sea.

SUBHI. Eli. Eli is there, in the sea. Waiting for us. Full of the
moon's secrets.

QUEENY *holds* SUBHI*'s hand.*

I'm sorry, brother. I'm so sorry, Eli. I'm so sorry.

They sit and watch the sea.

JIMMIE *enters, on the other side of the stage. She flashes*
her torch.

SUBHI *sees it, and flashes back.*

Both kids smile.

JIMMIE *keeps flashing her torch as she walks towards the camp.*

MAÁ *laughs.*

MAÁ. You know this torch person?

SUBHI....It's my friend, Jimmie.

MAÁ. Your friend knows Morse code.

SUBHI....What's she saying?

MAÁ (*translating the flashes*). Why did the chicken cross the road?

SUBHI *shakes his head. The flashes continue.*

To get to the idiot's house. Knock knock.

QUEENY (*joining in the fun*). Who's there?

MAÁ. The chicken.

They laugh.

That's a terrible joke.

JIMMIE *is coming closer.* SUBHI *climbs down to meet her.*

The lights focus on just SUBHI *and* JIMMIE.

JIMMIE. Thanks for saving me and all. Like a superhero. (*Laughs.*) Super-Subhi.

JIMMIE *takes the Bone Sparrow off her neck.*

It's your turn. To wear the Sparrow. For now, anyway.

SUBHI *shakes his head but* JIMMIE *passes the Bone Sparrow through the fence.*

I don't need its protection any more. Max from school said that I almost died so what kind of protection could it be, but I told him that he was wrong. I told him that the Bone Sparrow brought you to me, to save me. You need its protection now.

SUBHI *stares at the sea; hears* ELI*'s whale song.*

He nods, takes the Bone Sparrow through the fence holes, and puts it around his neck.

SUBHI. I see now. Thank you.

JIMMIE. What?

SUBHI. I don't have to wait for Someday. To weave the net.

JIMMIE. What are you talking about, Subhi?

Scene Seven

SUBHI *sits in a soulless room opposite an investigator,* ZARA. *He doesn't look at her while she talks, just draws and draws and draws on his paper. He wears the Bone Sparrow around his neck.*

ZARA. Subhi. You can relax, okay? This is just a chat… My name is Zara. I'm just asking everyone about what happened… that day. I've spoken to Beaver. He said that Eli was stirring up the protestors and that was why it grew into a riot. That they started destroying things, burning things, and that he and Harvey had no choice but to intervene. Then, Eli climbed onto the roof of one of the demountables. He had a weapon. A knife. He lunged from there at Beaver. He fell. Beaver tried to save him. Harvey tried to save him. But they couldn't. Is that what you saw happen?

SUBHI *doesn't say anything, only draws.*

Don't worry about anyone else. This is just between you, and me, okay?

SUBHI *doesn't say anything, only draws.*

DUCK. Of course, if you say what happened, Harvey's done for. Food for the fishes and all that. Because if you say what happened, then they'll have to ask why Harvey didn't say anything straight off. And they'll have to ask why Harvey didn't come back to help Eli. They'll say he is as guilty as Beaver. Then again, if you don't say anything, no one will know the truth about Eli. Or maybe your sister is right. Maybe no one cares. Maybe you don't really exist after all.

SUBHI *grabs the* DUCK *and throws him across the room.*

ZARA. Is everything alright?

SUBHI *hands* ZARA *the drawing. We see a hand-drawn animation of* ELI, *standing tall.*

SUBHI. It's important. What story we choose to tell. Nasir taught me that.

Beat.

We were supposed to be hot-chocolate chefs.

ZARA....I don't quite...

SUBHI *takes out* JIMMIE's *phone, and gives it to* ZARA.

SUBHI. You'll need this. Later.

ZARA....Okay.

SUBHI. Listen.

ZARA *gives* SUBHI *her full attention.*

Once there lived a kid in limbo called Eli. And this is his story.

Blackout.

The End.

Educational Resources, Exercises and Activities
Written by Imrana Mahmood and Carolyn Bradley,
and edited by Oliver O'Shea for Pilot Theatre

These resources are designed for educators who are teaching
The Bone Sparrow by Zana Fraillon within KS3 English and
PSHE curricula, or responding with their students to the
adaptation by S. Shakthidharan which they have either seen on
stage or read in this book.

The resources feature prompt questions, activities and ideas (all
in shaded panels like this) to encourage students to engage
creatively with some of the challenging issues and topics raised
by the novel and the play, enriching their learning outcomes.

We would suggest that you consider whether any of the subjects
explored in these resources may be triggering for some of your
students, especially if they have experience of seeking
sanctuary.

See more information and resources at www.pilot-theatre.com

Principal Characters

Subhi is the main protagonist of *The Bone Sparrow*. He is a nine-year-old Rohingya refugee born in an Australian detention centre. He lives with his Maá and sister Queeny. He has no experience of the outside world so relies on stories from family members. Subhi also has an active imagination which manifests itself through the 'Night Sea' and 'Shakespeare duck'.

Queeny's actual name is Noor, but only Maá calls her that. She is Subhi's older sister and, whilst supportive, she does not always entertain Subhi's imagination and sometimes struggles to share his sense of optimism. She works closely with Eli later on in the story, to ensure the outside community becomes aware of the conditions within the centre.

Maá fled the violence in Myanmar along with her husband and daughter Queeny. She lost her husband and ended up in the detention centre, where she gives birth to Subhi, and spends time telling him stories of their time in Myanmar before and after the persecution began. Eventually, Maá becomes quieter, more tired, not eating well and has to be monitored to ensure she does not become a danger to herself.

Jimmie lives with her father and brother Jonah. The family used to move around and initially came to the town close to the detention centre so Jimmie's dad could find work. Her mother died three years ago, and since then the mines have closed down and the town suffers high unemployment, so her father must rely on shift work outside of the town. Despite the fact they are still grieving for their loss, Jimmie has a Bone Sparrow necklace given to her by her mother as a symbol of unity and protection. One day Jimmie discovers a small notebook amongst her mother's possessions which she is unable to read, but she wants to keep it so that she has an ongoing connection to her mother's words and stories. Jimmie loves exploring and also has a pet rat called Raticus.

Eli lives in Family Tent Four of the detention centre. He has no family of his own, but he has a brotherly relationship with Subhi. Eli runs a 'package delivery business' inside the centre, where people can swap items with one another, and Subhi works with him to help him make deliveries to the different compounds. Eli's mother was killed by soldiers and his younger brother died in a truck. He is waiting to leave the centre once his uncle sends through the necessary paperwork, but this does not materialise and Eli ends up in Alpha Compound.

Harvey is one of the Jackets (detention guards) who treats the detainees better than other Jackets do. Harvey inadvertently introduces Subhi to 'Shakespeare duck' who becomes an imaginary but vital companion. Despite Harvey's seemingly compassionate attitude, he struggles to speak up for truth and justice at the end of the story.

Beaver is another of the Jackets at the detention centre, who was attacked by a detainee who had 'turned crazy and grabbed a hammer'. He treats the people inside the centre with contempt, lacking any compassion for them.

Context

The Rohingya People

Rohingya people are a Muslim ethnic-minority group living in
Myanmar, which is a majority Buddhist country in South-East
Asia, formerly known as Burma.

The Rohingya are not recognised by Myanmar as being an
official ethnic group on the census, so they are 'stateless' and
therefore vulnerable to exploitation, deportation and abuse.
Many Rohingya have fled to neighbouring Bangladesh and live
in overcrowded refugee camps.

Here, Sirazul Islam – Pilot Theatre's Assistant Director through
the Regional Theatre Young Director Scheme – shares his own
lived experience:

'The treatment of refugees is portrayed quite accurately in
The Bone Sparrow, especially since Subhi doesn't know how
he's supposed to be treated in the world, per se. He has some
ideas, but he hasn't lived in the outside world. And that's an
issue for many people in the refugee camps and in detention
centres around the world, including myself. I didn't know
when I was in a refugee camp that this was not how we were
supposed to be treated, because we hadn't seen life outside. I
was born in a refugee camp, and I spent my entire childhood
in a refugee camp.

For many of these people, it is quite hard for them to
recognise the difference between what life is supposed to be
and how it is, and their human rights. For example, the right
to medication, the right to education – we didn't know we
had these rights. We didn't know these rights existed.

A lot of people when they hear us speak, when they see that
we're in this situation, they think, "Oh, why didn't we
speak? How or why didn't we do this?" They try to put
themselves in our positions, in our shoes, and think, "Oh,

had I been in his position I would have done something different." And it's quite easy to say it – if you haven't been in that situation, if you don't know what life is like outside, what the norm is outside, what you've grown up in, outside what you've seen... Being a refugee, being a detainee, it's not a choice. It's what they've known.

When I first came to the UK, I just thought I was normal like everyone else. Until I started growing up, until I started realising all the violence that I saw was "normal", the people I saw detained were "normal", and then as I grew older, I started reading the news.

And then when it came to secondary school in England, people would ask, "Where are you from?", and I would say, "I'm from Burma, from Myanmar." And I get weird looks because no one knows where Burma is, no one knows where Myanmar is, and especially no one has ever heard of the Rohingya. It became very difficult for me to express my identity.

So, I would just tell them, "I'm a Bengali. I'm from Bangladesh." It made it much easier because people knew more. But as I grew up, I started struggling with my identity. I was born in a Bangladesh refugee camp, but Bangladesh has not accepted me. I am a Burmese, but the Burmese have not accepted me, and now I'm a British citizen. But there's a part of me that will never feel accepted because I was not born here, I'll never know what it really, truly means to belong to a homeland.

For Subhi, he grew up in the detention centre, he was born in Australia, but he's not an Australian, he would never be accepted as an Australian, because that's not what his identity is. His identity is a Rohingya Muslim, but even that is suppressed. Suppression of identity has always been used as a tool against us, not just to suppress our identity but to suppress any form of rebellion.

Subhi is a fictional character, but just like him there are thousands of teenagers and children in refugee camps and detention centres right now, who are in the same situation as him, who do not have the luxury to have seen the outside world, who do not have the luxury of seeing what life is supposed to be.

Subhi is not the story of one person. He is an embodiment of what is going around the world. The violence faced by not just the Rohingyas, but other minority groups is what Subhi shows. Nonetheless, this is a story of hope, ambition and rebellion. One that takes you on a journey that many have been on before, but not all of them have lived to tell it.

I am Subhi. You are Subhi. We are all Subhi.'

The following activities can help students engage further with, and relate to, Sirazul's story:

- Ask students to read aloud Sirazul's story, taking it in turns to help them engage with it. Encourage them to be active listeners and discuss what they have learnt afterwards.

- Ask students to select five key sentences and bring them to life through a still image or images. These can then be shared, perhaps with music, to create a short performance.

- As an extension of this task, students can add in a line from Sirazul's story to each image – they can experiment with vocal effects such as choral speaking, echo, ripple, cannon, unison or repetition to give each line dramatic effect.

- Sirazul's story can be used as a source for a short piece of verbatim theatre. Verbatim theatre, a form of documentary theatre, is made using the spoken words of real people, which are then brought to life on stage. Students can experiment with ways of bringing to life Sirazul's words through theatre, perhaps incorporating physical theatre, choral movement or speaking, or multimedia. This can be a starting point for a devised piece, or as a standalone exercise to help students engage further with the themes and context of *The Bone Sparrow*.

Themes

Sanctuary Seekers

The UN Refugee Agency (UNHRC) categorises sanctuary seekers in six main categories:

Asylum Seekers: An asylum seeker is an individual who is seeking international protection.

Internally Displaced People: The internally displaced seek safety in other parts of their country.

Refugees: Refugees are people fleeing conflict or persecution.

Stateless People: Stateless people do not have a nationality and can struggle to realise their human rights.

Returnees: Returnees are people who have finally returned home.

Safeguarding Individuals: Every human being deserves a life free from persecution and discrimination.

- Which of the six categories do the Rohingya people fall into?

'Most people have their Boat ID as their number. Maá is NAP-24 and Queeny is NAP-23. But I was born here so I have a different ID. DAR-1, that's me.' [Subhi]

- What does your name mean?
- Who named you?
- What do you like about your name?
- Do you have a nickname?
- How much of our identity is shaped by our names?
- Why do you think the refugees are identified with letters and numbers?
- What effect will identifying people in this way have?

- And what impact will this have on how they are viewed/treated by others?

- By refusing to refer to the refugees by name, how do the Jackets contribute to their dehumanisation?

'About every country in the world saying we don't belong. Not in this place. Not in any place.'

- Have you ever felt like you do not belong? Have you ever felt excluded or been made to feel like an outsider?

- International borders are a social and political construct, essentially meaning that they are the result of human decisions, interactions and conflicts. To what extent does the notion of borders create barriers for people seeking sanctuary and why?

- Who do you think should be responsible for giving a home to refugees?

- Whose responsibility is it to keep people safe and protected?

Detention Centres

The UNHCR Refugee Convention was set up in 1951 as an international agreement under which claims of asylum can be made. Claiming asylum means you fear danger in your own country so you seek protection and safety in a potential host country. The agreement states that a person must have a 'well-founded fear of persecution' – this means you are being specifically mistreated and targeted because of your identity or set of beliefs, such as your race, religion, nationality, political opinion or membership of a particular social group.

In the UK, the Home Office determines whether or not to accept or refuse asylum applications. If an application is upheld, then the person has permission to live in the community. However, if an application is denied then they could be subject to immigration control and detained. If they are detained under immigration powers, they will usually be held in a short-term holding facility and then moved longer term to a detention centre. People who are held in detention centres have limited freedom and cannot leave without permission. In the UK there is no time limit on how long someone can be detained, meaning a person can be detained indefinitely.

An example of a detention centre in the UK is Yarl's Wood located in Bedfordshire, which houses women and family groups awaiting immigration clearance. It was opened in 2001 and has been the subject of heavy criticism and numerous controversies ever since, including hunger strikes by detainees to protest inadequate treatment by staff, sexual abuse, and the detrimental impact of detaining children.

There have been two other main locations, Penally in Pembrokeshire (which closed in March 2021) and Folkestone in Kent, where ex-army barracks have been converted into temporary accommodation – but they have been described by human rights groups as 'unsanitary and unsuitable' and as being like 'a prison without the safeguards of a prison'.

The UN estimates that there are 26 million refugees around the world, and the UK has resettled around 26,000 refugees in the past five years. The World Bank puts the total number of refugees in the UK in 2018 at 127,000, or 0.5% of the world's refugees. In fact, the Red Cross reports that 'the majority of displaced people, 85%, now live in developing countries. And 73% are in neighbouring countries or places close to the country they have fled.'

- What responsibility does the international community have in responding to calls for help by those that are incarcerated?

- Queeny and Eli work together to visually document the conditions inside the centre, as well as the hunger-strike protest with the aim of being shared by the media. What role does the media play in the way in which refugees and asylum seekers are portrayed?

- Why are some governments allowing people to be incarcerated for long periods of time?

- What are your thoughts on identifying some human beings as 'illegal'? Who gets to decide who is illegal? Why might some governments choose to use such language? What impact does such language have on wider society?

- What might compel refugees/asylum seekers to go on hunger strike as a form of protest?

Sources: www.bbc.co.uk/news/uk-england-kent-56325360; www.freemovement.org.uk/statistics-refugees-uk; www.redcross.org.uk/about-us/what-we-do/how-we-support-refugees/find-out-about-refugees

Storytelling

'Maá says it's because I listen to the earth. She says if everyone would listen to the stories deep inside the earth, we would hear the whisperings of everything there is to hear, and if everyone did that, then just maybe we wouldn't all get stuck so much.'

- Do you feel that our society is less connected to nature?

- Do you think this lack of care for the world around us affects the way we treat each other?

- What might we learn if we were more attuned to our wider community?

'That was when Maá stopped talking to me in Rohingya too. She reckons that if I only speak in English, then no one will think I am any different when we get out.'

- How must Subhi feel knowing his mum thinks he should only speak in English?

- Why might Maá believe assimilation is the key to being accepted?

- Is it right to create an environment where we expect someone who is different to change/hide their identity to fit in?

Colonialism might be defined as 'control by one power over a dependent area or people' – and language is often used as a colonial tool: 'Colonisers imposed their languages and cultures by forcing non-Western people to learn to speak a different language.' (*Language and Colonization* by Sayeh Sayedayn)

- In light of this, how do schools view English as an Additional Language (EAL) students?

- Why do you think some people think it is a disadvantage to speak English as an additional language (even though this means they can already fluently speak a different language)?

- How much of this is rooted in colonial thinking?

'I keep on at Maá every night, asking her for a story. Just a single one. Because sometimes, in here, when people stop talking, and stop asking, and stop remembering, that's when they start to lose a piece of themselves.'

- How important is storytelling in preserving one's identity and culture?

'I need these stories. Everyone else in here has memories to hold on to. Everyone else has things to think on to stop them getting squashed down to nothing. But I don't have memories of anywhere else, and all these days just squish into the same. I need their stories. I need them to make my memories.'

- How important are stories in helping Subhi learn about his culture and heritage?

- Subhi was born in the detention centre. How might it feel for him not being able to share stories of the outside with his family and friends?

- Children growing up in detention centres may not have many positive experiences, so how might this affect their mental health? How might stories help with their wellbeing?

Friendship

'It doesn't matter that Eli's older than me by more than Queeny is; he's my best friend and we tell each other everything there ever is to tell. Eli says we're more than best friends. We're brothers.'

- Why do you think Eli and Subhi have such a strong bond?

- Eli loses his brother before coming to the centre. How does this impact Eli's relationship to Subhi?

- Despite having a brotherly connection, why do you think Subhi fails to help Eli when he is being attacked by Beaver?

'I can see the girl in my head. There is something in her that makes me feel that I've met her before.'

- What do Jimmie and Subhi have in common? How does this bring them closer together?

- How does Jimmie and Subhi's friendship help them cope with their own circumstances?

- What do you think Subhi and Jimmie gain from their friendship?

'All the kids like Harvey. Some of the other Jackets can be nice enough too, but not like Harvey. Usually the nice ones don't stay too long anyway. But Harvey's been here longer than me, even.'

- Why do you think Harvey is kinder than the other Jackets?

- How does Harvey treat Subhi?

- Why do you think Harvey struggles to save Eli or expose what Beaver did?

Imagination

*'Sometimes, at night, the dirt outside turns into a beautiful
ocean. As red as the sun and as deep as the sky.'*

- Subhi imagines the ocean to be red in colour. Why do you
  think he imagines the ocean to be this way? Subhi has never
  seen the world outside the fence, so he needs to rely on his
  imagination. Does an alternative perception of reality impact
  Subhi's understanding of the world?

- How does the Night Sea and the treasures Subhi finds help
  him feel connected to his father?

- Many detention centres are set up in locations unsuitable for
  long-term living, such as being susceptible to flooding. Do
  you think Subhi's imagination of the Night Sea is a way of
  coping with the harsh conditions in which he is living?

*'If us kids ran the world, there would be ice cream every day
and roast lamb with mint sauce and potatoes once a month, and
so much water that we could all drink until our stomachs were
just about to burst... and hot chocolate rain falling from the
sky.'*

- How does imagining the idea of a feast help Eli and Subhi
  deal with their living conditions inside the centre?

*'That's her! the Shakespeare duck quacks. I reckon he's more
excited than me. Don't forget to find out her name this time, he
reminds me. He's getting kind of bossy for a rubber duck.'*

- Why is the Shakespeare duck an important part of Subhi's
  everyday existence?

- How does the author use the duck to share insights into the
  story?

- Do you think it matters that Subhi does not know who
  Shakespeare is?

Deprivation

'There are only fourteen pairs of real shoes in this whole entire camp, even though there must be about nine hundred pairs of feet.'

'We've had food shortages for the last four days and have only been getting half scoops.'

'For a bit, a teacher came and taught everyone. But then the Jackets said it was too expensive and there were too many kids.'

'Even when Jimmie's dad lost his job along with the rest of the town, and had to find a new job working shifts, which took him away from home for days at a time. This is where their mum had been the happiest. And so they would stay. No one else would want to move into an empty town full of nothing but memories, anyway.'

- Why are the conditions inside the detention centre so poor?

- What are the different types of deprivation being experienced – e.g. food, money, knowledge, family?

- The Universal Declaration of Human Rights states different rights to which all human beings should be entitled. Which rights are Subhi and other refugees being denied?

Workshops and Activities

Workshop: Identity

Who Am I?

Ask the students to sit in a circle (with a large sheet of paper in the centre), and ask them to answer the following questions in pairs:

- What is your name?
- Who named you?
- What does your name mean?
- Do you have a nickname?
- Do you like/dislike your name and why?
- Invite a few students to the centre of the circle to write their name on the paper and share the answers to the questions.

Who Are You?

- Hand out two slips of blank paper to each student, and ask everyone to write down three words to describe themselves on the paper slip and put into a container (e.g. a pouch, hat, basket...).
- Everyone gets into pairs, and decides who will be Person A and who will be Person B.
- Next, Person A and B both write down three words on a slip to describe each other and put them into another container.
- The pairs swap containers and slips of paper, then take out the slips from both containers to compare and discuss.
- Working in groups of three or four pairs, students should discuss: How were they perceived by their partners and how did that compare with their own description?

- Each group should identify a 'scribe' to note down keywords from the discussion on large sheets of paper.

- They should also identify one 'spokesperson' to feed back to the rest of the students.

- The whole group should come back into a circle and feed back.

Hotseating

- Set up a chair at the front of the room and ask all the students to sit facing the chair.

- Ask a volunteer to sit on the chair and to choose one of the characters from the story.

- Other students can then ask the 'character' a series of questions like an interview or Q&A. For example, a student playing Subhi could be asked how he feels being called DAR-1? How important is the Night Sea to him? What does he like most about drinking hot chocolate? And so on.

- The student playing the character must improvise the answers by imagining what the character might say. There are no right or wrong answers, but should be as true to the character and the story as possible.

Workshop: Storytelling

The Power of Memories

'I need these stories. Everyone else in here has memories to hold on to. Everyone else has things to think on to stop them getting squashed down to nothing. But I don't have memories of anywhere else, and all these days just squish into the same. I need their stories. I need them to make my memories.' [Subhi]

'No one else would want to move into an empty town full of nothing but memories, anyway. But Jimmie likes exploring memories.' [Jimmie]

Discuss the role that memories play in the lives of Subhi and Jimmie.

Next, ask the students to lie on the floor with their eyes closed, and then asks them to imagine a place, with a guided series of questions linked to their five senses. Let's use the example of a beach.

Sight

- What can you see?
- What is the ground like?
- What colours can you see around you?
- What time of day is it?
- Are there other people on the beach? If so, what are they doing?
- What are you wearing? Are you wearing a cap or sunglasses?
- Are you lying down and looking up at the sky or are you sitting up and looking out at the horizon?
- Maybe you are lying down on a lounger underneath a colourful parasol?

Sound

- What can you hear?
- Can you hear the waves of the sea?
- What does your breathing sound like?
- What does it sound like when you move around?
- Have you found a big seashell and put it next to your ear? Can you hear the whirling and whishing sound of the sea?

Taste

- What can you taste?
- Are you hungry?
- Have you packed a picnic with you? If yes, what have you got?
- Pick one thing and eat it. Is it sweet or savoury? Do you like it?

- Have you brought an ice cream? How sweet is it? Is it melting in the sun?
- Can you taste the salty air?

Touch

- What can you feel?
- What does the ground feel like under your feet?
- Are you barefoot and can you feel the soft grainy texture of the sand in between your toes?
- Does the sand feel warm?
- Or maybe you are taking a stroll along the beach. Can you feel the cold wet sand beneath your feet?
- How does it feel when a small wave crashes on to the shore, immersing your feet? Is the water cold? Do you feel refreshed?
- Have you found a small seashell? What does it feel like in your hands?

Smell

- What can you smell?
- Can you smell the seaweed left by the waves on the beach?
- Does the air smell fresh?
- Or maybe you can smell a slight sweaty odour from your body?
- Can you smell the different foods from your picnic?

Workshop: The Power of the Image

The Power of Photographs

'And then the pictures are all outside. I see trees and rivers and rocks and nests and roads and tracks leading to more and more of Outside. Jimmie tells me about each and every one, and what we'll do and asks where I'd like to go first.'

Ask the students to bring in a photograph of themselves which is of sentimental value. A screenshot or printout of the photo may be safest, rather than the only copy of a precious family photo!

Ask the students to write a description of the memory prompted by the photograph through a free-writing exercise.

Exodus

'It's not what you look at that matters. It's what you see.'
[Henry David Thoreau]

Visit this link to see some Pulitzer Prize-winning photographs of the Rohingya crisis: reut.rs/3HATppn. Please note that all of these photographs are very hard-hitting and distressing, and you may particularly wish to avoid Images 9 to 13 which depict people who have died.

Sharing some of these images with your students, discuss the following questions:

- What do you think is meant by political photography?

- Do you think political photography is important? Why?

- What impact does photography have on politics?

- To what extent does political photography influence the way a crisis is reported/received?

- What might be some ethical implications for the photographer?

- What emotions does Image 1 evoke?

- Does Image 2 enhance your understanding of the violence committed by the Myanmar army?

- Do you think the photographer who took Images 7 and 8 would have done anything to help the people fleeing from violence?

- The caption for Image 14 states the Rohingya refugees crossed illegally into Bangladesh. How much responsibility and influence does the media have in how they describe their images?

- Reuters was awarded a Pulitzer Prize for documenting the Rohingya crisis. What are your feelings on an outsider receiving recognition whilst those they photograph are suffering?

- Can political photography be a vehicle for justice?

Freeze-frames

'The people out there will remember us. Soon they'll see that living here isn't living at all. We just need to show them who we are, that we're people, and then they'll remember. This time, they won't forget.'

Ask the students to curate a freeze-frame – like their own still photograph – which represents something about *The Bone Sparrow*. They should pick a theme they want to explore; objects and subjects they wish to use; and a message they want to convey through the image.

Next, ask the students to get into small groups, and then call out different sections of the novel or play, allowing them ten seconds to create a freeze-frame which represents that part of the story. Here are some examples from Chapter 19 of the novel:

- Eli and Subhi kneeling down near the fence, both are sad and crying; Subhi holding Eli's hand through the fence.

- Men lying down, lips sewn shut; Eli standing with them holding a sheet that says 'WE ARE INNOCENT. PLEASE HELP US TO BE FREE. WE CAN'T LIVE WITHOUT HOPE.'

- Eli and the other men facing Queeny. Queeny standing with a camera. Eli and the man holding the sheet facing the camera.

- Jimmie sitting with her dad, looking at the newspaper with the photograph of the men taken by Queeny.

- Jimmie and Eli sitting together, surrounded by food, talking about the image in the newspaper.

- Jackets forcibly pouring water down the throat of a man on hunger strike.

- Subhi digging down into the dirt with his hands and discovering a knife.

Ask the students to showcase their freeze-frames, and explain the reasons for their chosen image.

Alternatively, ask them to draw a comic strip or series of illustrations to represent the freeze-frames.

Workshop: Journalism

Story Circle

- Ask the students to sit in a circle and each student to take it in turns to say one sentence as part of the story. For example:

  STUDENT 1. Once there was a rubber duck...

  STUDENT 2....who was a magic duck and could talk.

  STUDENT 3. The duck loved to drink hot chocolate...

  STUDENT 4....but one day the hot chocolate ran out.

  STUDENT 5. So the duck became really sad and started drinking coffee instead...

And so on.

Newspaper Article

- Ask the students to write a newspaper article which sheds light on the issues faced by the people in the detention centre:

- What is the specific story they want to write about?

- What heading will they use?

- How will they begin the first sentence for their opening paragraph?

- What words will they include to convey empathy?

- What kind of image will they use for the article?

Interviews

- Ask the students, if they were a journalist, who would they like to interview and why.

- Ask them to write down a list of three questions they would ask during the interview.

- Compare and discuss with the group.

Writing Prompts

Here are some prompts for students to write autobiographically or creatively.

- Imagine a place where you feel free, either now or when you were aged nine.

- What are your childhood memories? Has your life changed since then – and how?

- What are your family members' childhood memories? Where did they live? How have their lives changed since they were children?

- Do you have any family stories which have been passed down from generation to generation?

- Are there any stories about your family or neighbourhood which you would like to be passed on to future generations?

- Think about the way in which the people inside detention centres have been forgotten by the world. Write an acrostic poem using words such as 'REMEMBER' or 'FREEDOM'.

- Subhi grew up in the detention centre and does not know what the outside world is like. Imagine if Subhi were going to come from the detention centre to live with you and your family. What sorts of things would you introduce him to and why?

- Subhi uses 'Someday' as a method of staying strong, he looks to what his future will be. Write your Someday story: 'Someday, I will…'

Drama Activities

The following exercises can be used to introduce students to the
themes and plot of *The Bone Sparrow* before they watch or read
the play, or can be used during the study of the play to deepen
understanding.

You could pick and choose from these activities or put them
together for a longer workshop. You will need Post-its, pens,
paper, copies of the poem and key quotes printed out.

Still Images

Put students into groups and ask them to create still images
based on each of the following words: *Heritage*, *Imagination*,
Discrimination, *Hope*, *Deportation*, *Asylum*, *Prejudice*,
Journey, *Family*, *Friendship*, *Refuge*.

The still images could be literal or abstract. Encourage students
to experiment with levels, space, physicality, and contact work.
The images could be performed to music to create an emotive
piece of physical theatre.

Dramatising a Rohingya Poem

Read the following poem taken from the script. It is spoken in
Ruáingga (the Rohingya language) by Ba, Subhi's father. In
groups, ask students to dramatise the poem through still images
or improvisation.

> 'Life is an open prison
> We can see the sky and stars
> We can feel the breeze
> But we can never fly away
> The sky is the limit
> Yet we are the ground
> But I can still breathe the air of my motherland as it
>   sweeps through the clouds
> One day we will grow wings and ride upon it.'

Interpreting Quotes

In groups, give students one of these following quotes from the
play. Ask students to discuss the quote, thinking about what it
could mean and why it is significant.

Students can either feed back their thoughts to the group or use the quote as a stimulus for an improvised scene, building on their understanding of the play's themes.

'Sometimes, at night, the dirt outside turns into a beautiful ocean. The Night Sea. As red as the sun and as deep as the sky.' [Subhi]

'I'm gonna see the sea. Feel it. Taste it. The real sea, someday. When me and Maá and Queeny are free.' [Subhi]

'There are fourteen pairs of real shoes in this whole entire camp, and close to nine hundred pairs of feet.' [Eli]

'You're nineteen fence diamonds high now, right?' [Eli]

'Every one of your drawings is a story, Subhi. A kind of blanket to wrap yourself up in and keep you safe.' [Harvey]

'I don't have memories of anywhere else, and all these days just squish into the same. I need their stories. I need them to make my memories.' [Subhi]

Setting the Scene

In advance of this exercise, ask students to research images of detention centres and the Australian outback, and to prepare a design moodboard to bring to the session. Explain to students that the setting of the play is '*a detention centre in the remote Australian desert*' and the opening stage directions describe '*the dusty red earth of the Australian outback*'.

With this information, ask students to sketch a set design which could be used for a production of the play. As an extra challenge, you could ask students to consider different styles of design – a naturalistic design, a Brechtian design, a design using multimedia, or designs for different configurations of stage (end-on, in the round, traverse, promenade...).

Walk the Space

Ask students to get into pairs, and label themselves A and B. A should close their eyes, and B should guide them carefully around the space. Whilst B is guiding, they should narrate the space they see around them, imagining it is the setting of the play: '*a detention centre in the remote Australian desert*'. B should describe what they can see in as much detail as possible, and A should try to visualise this. Partners can then swap and try the exercise again.

Researching Rohingya Folk Tales

Stories and storytelling are a central theme of the play, and Rohingya folk tales, poems and music are interwoven throughout the narrative. Students can either research a Rohingya folk tale to use as a stimulus for a piece of devised work, or they could research a folk tale from any heritage, perhaps something which has been passed down in their own family through the oral tradition.

Key Moments

After students have read or seen the play, ask them to split the story into ten key moments, which they can write on Post-its or paper. Once they have established their ten key moments, they can then develop each moment into a still image, and then work on transitions between each image.

Day in the Life

Using their knowledge of the play, ask students to write down on large pieces of paper what an average day in the camp would look like for Subhi. Where does he go? Who does he see? What does he do? And so on.

Ask your students to write down what an average day in their own lives would look like, to prompt discussion about the challenges some people face and the inequality which exists in the world.

Letter-writing

Ask students to imagine they are one of the characters in the play, and to write a letter in role to another character. Examples of letters they could write are: Subhi writing to Ba, Jimmie writing to her mum or dad, Maá writing to Ba.

Students can then develop their writing in character into short monologue performances or devised group pieces.

Untold Stories

Students can consider the characters in the play whom we know less about, and deepen their understanding of these characters through improvisation work.

They might think about the backstories of Harvey, Nasir, Ba, Eli or Beaver, and develop short improvisations to show these characters' lives outside of the play.

Journeys

Journeys, both literal and figurative, are a key aspect of *The Bone Sparrow*. Ask students to think about the journey Subhi's family would have had to make from Myanmar to Australia, and the conditions they may have travelled in.

Students can look at maps in atlases or online to research the route and the treacherous journeys that asylum seekers make. This research can then be used as a stimulus for a piece of devising on the theme of journeys.

Shadow Puppetry

The story of Oto and Anka is told through mask, puppetry and movement in the play. Students could retell a section of this story through simple shadow puppetry – using a white sheet, card puppets, and a strong torch.

Staging the Fire

The climax of the narrative is a fire that spreads through the camp and the ensuing chaos. Ask students to think about ways of staging this complex section of the text. The following stage directions could be used as a starting point:

- *'Queeny and Eli, caked in sweat, set fire to two different parts of the stage. This act is done with reverence, urgency and rage. They are fed up. This is their protest.'*

- *'Over the course of the scene, the smoke grows and takes over the stage.'*

- *'The yelling grows, the sound of fire and things breaking grows.'*

- *'The sound of the riots grow and grow. There are more scuffles.'*

- *'The riots break open the set. Scuffles with detainees break down fences. The stage becomes a mess.'*

To stage this part of the action, students could use physical theatre, soundscapes, coloured fabric, multimedia, lighting and sound – or whatever resources they have available to them. Encourage them to be as imaginative as possible.

Epilogue

The play ends with Subhi talking to Zara, an investigator, as he tells her what happened in the camp. Ask your students to stage an epilogue scene, which continues Subhi's story. Here are some ideas for scene work:

- Show what happens to Subhi or Queeny after the play has ended.

- Show a scene between Subhi and Jimmie after the play has ended.

- Develop a scene showing an interview between Zara and Harvey.

- Start a scene using the final line of the play – *'Once there lived a kid in limbo called Eli. And this is his story'* – and to tell the story of the play from Eli's perspective.

Adapting for the Stage

There are differences between Zana Fraillon's original novel and the stage play by S. Shakthidharan. In these activities, you can explore with students what it means to adapt a novel for the stage.

Prompt Questions

- How many other plays have you seen which were adaptations? Your students may be surprised how many plays or musicals were once novels. Some famous creative adaptations include *War Horse*, *The Woman in Black*, *Phantom of the Opera*, *Frankenstein*, *Les Misérables*...

- What are the differences in writing for the page and writing for the stage?

- What challenges does a playwright face when adapting a novel?

Further Activities

- If students have read the novel of *The Bone Sparrow*, ask them to list some of the major differences between the novel and the play, and then discuss why these differences are there.

- Ask your students to read the novel as home-learning over a couple of weeks.

- Ask your students to sketch their own idea of where the novel is set.

- Focus on a key scene in the novel and put students into groups to design this scene – with different responsibilities such as lighting, sound, set, costume and puppetry. Ask them to present their ideas back, explaining their dramatic intentions and the challenges and opportunities they faced.

- Ask your students to discuss the character of Subhi – and if the impressions they had from the novel are similar to how he was presented in the play.

- If watching the production, ask your students to discuss how the elements of staging such as puppetry, lighting, sound, set and costume brought the story to life.

Extended Activities

Students can creatively adapt their own scene from *The Bone Sparrow*. They will need to devise or write a script, and also design the set, lighting, sound and costume, depending on facilities, time and resources available.

Students can use creative adaptation as a devising project. Inspired by *The Bone Sparrow*, and thinking about the creative ways in which it has been adapted, they can adapt their own choice of novel, short story, poem or song for the stage.

Activism and Social Change

The purpose of activism is to bring about societal change through positive action. Many activists are passionate about social, economic and political issues, and invest a lot of time and effort to ensure they are creating platforms to challenge the status quo.

Activism can be achieved in myriad ways, including demonstrations and protests, striking, petitions, boycotts and social media campaigns. There are different examples of activism highlighted in *The Bone Sparrow*, such as hunger strikes. Ultimately, activism is also an act of defiance which can be embedded in an organisational structure by having a manifesto.

Here are two writing exercises to try with your students to engage their activist ideals.

Write a Manifesto

A manifesto is a statement that acts as a declaration of your vision, your intentions, core values and beliefs, what you stand for, or how you intend to live your life. It functions both as a statement of principles and as a call to action to achieve a revolutionary effect.

Plan and write a Young People's Manifesto to support the work of a human rights organisation (such as Amnesty International).

You could look at the Holstee Manifesto for inspiration: www.holstee.com/pages/manifesto

Here are some starting points:

- What do you believe in?
- What gets you out of bed in the morning (in the metaphorical sense)?
- What inspires you?
- What do you value most in the world?
- What change do you want to see in the world?

Here are some tips on writing your manifesto:

- Identify your 'why': Why are you wanting to make a change?
- Focus on the 'who': Whose problems are you trying to solve, to make lasting change?

Contact Your MP

The role of a Member of Parliament is to act in the national interest as well as reflect and represent the views of their constituents. The duties of an MP include scrutinising government policies and raising the profile of an issue in the media.

Knowing that MPs have the power, privilege and platform to bring the plight of the Rohingya into national (and international) conversations, what would be the advantage of writing a letter to your MP?

Plan and write a letter to your MP about refugees, the way in which they are treated, and what you would like your MP/the government to do? You can use the following as a template:

Dear < MP name >   < Date >

My name is < insert name here > and I'm writing to you today about < issue >. As a young person, this issue is extremely important to me because < reasons/your experiences >.

I would like you to < clear actions points for the MP to take away with them and a timeline on when you expect the issue to be resolved >.

Please respond to my letter and outline the steps you intend to take to address my concerns. If applicable, please escalate my letter to the relevant parliamentarian or department and keep me informed of any progress.

I look forward to hearing your response in due course.

Yours sincerely,
< Name >
< Full address including postcode >

Resources and Links

These resources and links might be of interest for you or your students to explore *The Bone Sparrow* and its themes further.

Pilot Theatre are not responsible for the content of external links, resources or books – and we strongly recommend checking the suitability of external content before sharing with your students.

Resources for Teaching *The Bone Sparrow*

www.amnesty.org.uk/resources/book-and-activities-bone-sparrow

literacytrust.org.uk/resources/bone-sparrow-teaching-resource

www.englishandmedia.co.uk/publications/emc-teaching-a-novel-the-bone-sparrow-download

Websites on Rohingya Culture

rohingyaculturalmemorycentre.iom.int

rohingyafolktales.com

musicinexile.org/bangladesh

Books on Rohingya Culture

First, They Erased Our Name: A Rohingya Speaks
by Habiburahman, with Sophie Ansel, translated by Andrea Reece

I Am a Rohingya: Poetry from the Camps and Beyond
edited and introduced by James Byrne and Shehzar Doja

I Am A Refugee by Tishya Kumar

Human Flow: Stories from the Global Refugee Crisis
by Ai Weiwei, including interviews with Rohingya people

Websites About Refugees and Sanctuary Seekers

www.unicef.org/emergencies/rohingya-crisis

www.redcross.org.uk/about-us/what-we-do/how-we-support-refugees/find-out-about-refugees

www.refugeecouncil.org.uk

cityofsanctuary.org

www.amnesty.org/en/what-we-do/refugees-asylum-seekers-and-migrants

www.unicef.org/emergencies/rohingya-crisis